THE G. STANLEY HALL LECTURE SERIES

Volume 3

G. STANLEY HALL, 1844–1924

THE G. STANLEY HALL LECTURE SERIES

Volume 3

Edited by
C. James Scheirer
and
Anne M. Rogers

1982 HALL LECTURERS

Florence L. Denmark
Rochel Gelman
K. E. Moyer
Irwin G. Sarason
Paul W. Thayer

AMERICAN PSYCHOLOGICAL ASSOCIATION
WASHINGTON, D.C.

99979

Published by the American Psychological Association, Inc.
1200 Seventeenth Street, N.W., Washington, DC 20036
Copyright © 1983 by the American Psychological Association.
All rights reserved.

ISBN: 0-912704-87X

Copies may be ordered from:
Order Department
American Psychological Association
1200 Seventeenth Street, N.W.
Washington, DC 20036

Printed in the United States of America

CONTENTS

PREFACE

S ince 1980 the G. Stanley Hall Lecture Series has sought to bring the best thinking in the field of psychology to the attention of the undergraduate instructor. The annual series consists of five lectures, each devoted to a different topic commonly covered in the introductory psychology course, presented at the annual meeting of the American Psychological Association (APA) and subsequently published as a single bound volume.

This book, the third volume of the Hall Series, includes the five lectures originally presented at the 1982 meeting of the APA in Washington, DC. The distinguished authors and their topics are Paul W. Thayer, industrial/organizational psychology; Florence L. Denmark, psychology of women; Irwin G. Sarason, abnormal psychology; K. E. Moyer, physiology; and Rochel Gelman, cognition. These authors were chosen, after a lengthy selection process, for their mastery of a particular content area, their strong interest in teaching psychology, their experience in teaching introductory psychology, and their understanding of the special problems inherent in teaching introductory psychology.

The instructor of the introductory psychology course faces an ever more formidable task. As the field of psychology splits into more and more specialty areas, it is hardly plausible for a single instructor to attempt to stay current in the many areas surveyed by the introductory course. Yet it is the introductory course within which most future psychologists and much of the college-educated population have their first taste of psychology. For those who do not major in the field, the course may be their only systematic exposure to the science and the profession.

These were the issues faced by the APA Committee on Undergraduate Education (CUE) at its meeting of March 1979. As the group responsible for implementing APA's concerns with the undergraduate curriculum, CUE recognized the plight of the introductory course instructor, who may teach 20 to 25 topics within a single course, and looked for ways to be of practical assistance.

The result was a proposal for a lecture series that would consist of 25 lectures, each covering a different topic, presented over a five-year period. Twenty topics were identified as the common subject matter of the introductory course, and four of these were scheduled each year. The fifth lecture each year was to examine a special topic chosen to reflect contemporary interest. To be sure these lectures reached those for whom they were intended, a two-step process was proposed: the five lectures would be presented at the annual meeting of the APA, and then published as an annual APA separate.

The parent board of CUE, APA's Education and Training Board, considered and approved the proposal. Many other groups and individuals contributed to the final shape of the proposal as it worked its way through the APA governance structure: the Committee on Continuing Education, the Board of Convention Affairs, the Division of Teaching of Psychology, and a number of individuals who were leaders in undergraduate psychology education.

The first paper in this volume is by Paul W. Thayer, who begins his review of industrial/organizational (I/O) psychology with the observation that the standard introductory text gives a median of two sentences to the subject. In addition, many of those who teach introductory psychology have read little beyond those two sentences, despite the fact that I/O psychology deals with an issue central to our personal and social lives—working. Research in I/O psychology looks at all aspects of working, from the job search through selection, training, designing jobs, compensation, career paths, to retirement. For this paper, Thayer chose those elements of the field that would matter the most to the introductory psychology student soon to enter the world of work: the selection process, entering organizations, job satisfaction and motivation, challenging assignments, individual training and development, and leadership. In his review of the literature in each area, Thayer looks at changing trends and common misassumptions, such as the notion that the unstructured interview is an effective way to select employees. He mentions fascinating new developments such as the "realistic job preview" and its impact on turnover, and growing cooperation between labor unions and I/O psychologists. He concludes with an injunction that readers understand that these elements of working interact with and modify one another.

Florence L. Denmark begins her paper, as did Thayer, with an informal survey of the textbook situation, which produced results she finds most disappointing. Denmark observes that although the most recently published texts do provide some coverage of the psychology of women, their approach—both in selecting topics and in the quality of treatment—is biased and unbalanced. To remedy this situation, Denmark argues for mainstreaming information about the psychology of women throughout the introductory course and textbook. This would, ideally, be supplemented by a unit and a chapter exclusively directed to scholarship about the psychology of women. To demonstrate how this could be done, Denmark discusses six issues related to the psychology of women, which she feels fit well into the main units of the introductory course: the women of psychology, methodological issues, moral development from a feminist perspective, biological foundations of behavior and sex differences, personality and mental health issues, and women and social behavior. Within each area, Denmark indicates common biases and errors and draws on recent research to present a balanced analysis of each issue.

In the third paper, Irwin G. Sarason achieves a comprehensive synthesis of the theoretical perspectives that currently guide research and clinical practice in abnormal psychology, and provides examples of the application of these principles. The four dominant theories are the biological theory, or the role of bodily processes; the psychodynamic theory, or the role of anxiety and inner conflict; the learning theory, or the role of the environment; and the cognitive theory, or the role of thinking and problem solving. A major theme of Sarason's paper is the interaction among the variables emphasized by the different theoretical perspectives—how each perspective may have something to contribute to our understanding of any particular case of abnormal behavior. With this theme in mind, Sarason reviews current research and concepts in four clinical groupings—depression, schizophrenia, anxiety disorders, and psychophysiological reactions. An increasing convergence among theorists of different perspectives is indicated by this review, although there is by no means unanimity among theorists. Stepping aside from theory, Sarason briefly examines the growing importance of behavioral medicine and health psychology, and the characteristics of the DSM III. He concludes with the hope that his manner of presentation establishes a structure that will help the student organize the subject matter of abnormal psychology in a meaningful and insightful fashion.

K. E. Moyer examines physiological psychology by thoroughly considering one aspect of the field: the physiology of aggression. From the research, he constructs a "model" of aggressive behavior based on the premise that the brains of animals and humans contain neural systems that are set off in the presence of certain stimuli, producing aggressive behavior or hostile feelings. Noting that aggression is not common in either animals or humans, Moyer poses the question to be answered: What turns on and what turns off the neural systems for aggression? He then discusses the research on those variables that determine whether the threshold for firing the neural systems in an individual is high or low in response to similar provocation. A predisposition toward aggression is apparently inherited in some cases. Blood chemistry, specifically hormonal and sugar levels, can have a dramatic effect on behavior. Therapeutic interventions, both cognitive and physiological, are now possible, bringing with them a host of profound ethical questions. We have the technology to reduce human aggression by electrical stimulation of specific areas in the brain or by lesioning the brain, but neither the serious physical side effects nor the ethical questions raised by Moyer have been sufficiently contemplated.

The fifth and final paper in this series is Rochel Gelman's all-inclusive commentary on cognitive development, the study of which Gelman argues is uncovering the universals of cognition, the nature of the workings of the human mind. Gelman opens with a summary of the main points of her paper, which exemplifies the breadth of her analysis. She then reviews traditional theories and recent research in cognitive development, and the apparent contradictions to which these give rise. This becomes a close look at a currently dominant trend within the field: the study of structures that are invariant throughout development. Gelman synthesizes a wealth of material from research to explain what the structures of development are, and how these evolve. Cognitive capacities exist at a very young age, and apparently guide development, much of which is self-motivated. Steps along the intricate path of cognitive development include gaining control over performance constraints, developing access and metacognition, inducing new principles, constructing knowledge systems, and differentiating and integrating structures and concepts.

Much appreciation is due to the authors, who fulfilled their difficult assignments in a masterful fashion that makes for excellent reading. The editors would also like to thank the many other individuals who contributed to the 1982 G. Stanley Hall Lecture Series and to the publication of this volume. Ludy T. Benjamin, Jr., Clyde Crego, Lucia A. Gilbert, Janet Matthews, Charles G. Morris, and R. Steven Schiavo were members of the advisory committee that selected the 1982 Hall lecturers. The editors also wish to thank the many individuals who commented on the original manuscripts from which this volume was produced. Special thanks are extended to Ellen Dykes and Deanna Cook, who shepherded the book through the many stages to final production. And finally, we want to thank former APA staff members Ludy T. Benjamin, Jr. and Kathleen D. Lowman, who worked so hard to make the G. Stanley Hall Lecture Series a reality.

C. James Scheirer and Anne M. Rogers

PAUL W. THAYER

INDUSTRIAL/ ORGANIZATIONAL PSYCHOLOGY: SCIENCE AND APPLICATION

Paul W. Thayer has been professor and head of the psychology department at North Carolina State University since 1977. Prior to 1977 he rose from a position in training research to senior vice-president at the Life Insurance Marketing and Research Association, a nonprofit association that provides research and education for the life insurance business. He has taught at the University of Pennsylvania and at Ohio State University, where he received his doctorate. He has consulted for federal and local governments, school systems, and large and small businesses. He is the author and co-author of many scientific articles and a book, *Training in Business and Industry.*

Thayer is a fellow of the American Association for the Advancement of Science (AAAS) and the American Psychological Association (APA), former president of APA's Division of Industrial/Organizational Psychology, and former chair of the APA Policy and Planning Board.

INDUSTRIAL/ ORGANIZATIONAL PSYCHOLOGY: SCIENCE AND APPLICATION

A person's happiness and self-esteem, from early childhood on, depend on a sense of accomplishment and achievement—a sense of doing at least one or two things in life very well. Because the average adult person in our society spends about half of his or her waking life at work, work is an important source of accomplishment and achievement. At the same time, society depends both on its citizens and on its organizations for productive activity; without such activity, society fails.

Industrial/organizational (I/O) psychologists are concerned with both individuals and organizations. American business, industry, and government are turning increasingly to I/O psychologists and job prospects are currently better in I/O psychology than in most areas of psychology. It is evident that I/O psychology has become an increasingly important field.

When I was approached to give this lecture I accepted at face value the instruction to "provide a content update in various fields of

The author expresses his appreciation to the more than 30 I/0 psychologists who made suggestions as to areas demanding coverage in this lecture. He is especially grateful to several colleagues who read earlier drafts and made helpful suggestions: Olga Engelhardt, Irv Goldstein, Milt Hakel, Jim Kalat, Bill McGehee, Bob Perloff, and Bjorg Thayer. All may regret that all suggestions were not heeded.

psychology." Being a department head whose only undergraduate teaching consists of an occasional guest lecture, I naively assumed that an important field like I/O psychology, which deals with such important personal and societal issues, would be amply covered in all introductory courses. My job of providing a content update would consist merely of describing some recent changes and trends in the field. To my surprise, however, a survey of 41 standard introductory texts on faculty shelves in our department revealed that the median "coverage" of I/O psychology consisted of two sentences (Kalat, Note 1).

Furthermore, in contrast to my own institution, where two I/O psychologists consistently teach introductory psychology, I discovered by talking to a few colleagues at other institutions that the vast majority of introductory psychology courses are taught by experimental or social psychologists, whose own contact with I/O psychology may not extend beyond the two sentences they read when they were students taking introductory psychology.

I shall therefore assume that my readership is composed of dutiful, possibly masochistic introductory psychology instructors, who probably know less about I/O psychology than they do about nude encounter therapy and consider it about as exciting as statistics. I sincerely hope that I can make the experience palatable, and I will try to make it even interesting.

There are over 2,000 fellows, members, and associates of APA in Division 14, the Division of Industrial and Organizational Psychology, soon to be the Society for Industrial and Organizational Psychology, Division 14 of APA. That's almost 4 percent of APA membership. Like the rest of APA, we are predominantly white and male, but the growth rate in women's membership since 1978 exceeds that of APA as a whole (Howard, Note 2). We are trying to attract more minorities.

We view ourselves as scientist-practitioners and have placed considerable stress on a strong scientific education in our *Guidelines for Doctoral Level Training in I/O Psychology* (APA Division 14, Note 3). Although in our early days we tended to offer our scientific and practitioner skills only to business, industry, government, and the military, we now also include labor, public, academic, community, and health organizations. About a third of us are primarily employed by business or industry, a third by academe, almost 10 percent by government, and about 20 percent by research or consulting organizations. Career outlooks are generally good in all sectors, although deep recessions can result in temporary dislocations for those in personnel work or research. (People concerns and research seem to go first in the face of financial adversity.)

We specialize in a wide variety of activities: selection, placement, management assessment, performance evaluation, job attitudes, motivation, training, career planning and development, organizational development, team-building, job redesign, environmental design, optimizing human-machine systems, safety, consumer behavior, advertising research, and so forth. We look to differential, experimental, and social psychology as our primary roots. We wish to enhance the quality of life for the individual at work and for the consumer as well as to make the organization more effective. We want to enhance the productive output of individuals, but we are also very much concerned with their ability to gain considerable satisfaction from their day-to-day activities. We may restructure the organization, modify compensation systems, redesign the work or the work place itself, or do a number of other things that would make both the individual and the work group more effective in both personal and organizational terms.

Because of the multiplicity of our activities, our backgrounds, and the places where we work, one might wonder what unites I/O psychologists under a single label. It is our concern with research and application in the world of work. Actually, the compound name has bothered us a good bit, but we have not been able to come up with a good substitute. There is not a lot of appeal in a title like, "work psychologists" or "psychologists of work." Certainly other psychologists would resent our calling ourselves "working psychologists." The use of either industrial or organizational offends those who have differing backgrounds in either differential and experimental psychology or social psychology.

That is a quick peek at the field. Students who are interested in this area can get a brochure prepared by Division 14 called, *A Career in Industrial/Organizational Psychology*, by writing to APA in Washington, DC. APA's annual *Graduate Study in Psychology and Associated Fields* lists I/O psychology programs. Division 14 also publishes a more detailed listing that includes graduate programs taught in business or organizational behavior departments or schools.[1] End of commercial. Now I will start getting to the details.

Research in I/O psychology has impact on all aspects of working life, from the beginning of the job search, through selection, training, designing jobs, compensation systems, career paths, and retirement. It affects safety, product designs, consumer opinion, and advertising. It touches on so many different areas that it will be impossible to treat all areas or to discuss more than a handful in any depth. In selecting those to be covered, I employed several criteria. The subject matter should be of interest or be relevant to introductory psychology students, be considered important by a number of some 30 prominent I/O psychologists I consulted, include some new developments of practical or theoretical interest, and help to illustrate the scientist-practitioner mode. No illustration will meet all these criteria, but each will meet the first and at least one other.

[1]Copies of the first two documents are available from APA; the latter costs $4.00. The third document is available from the current Division 14 Secretary-Treasurer.

I have one final comment before I start. I must consider each area as a separate entity and ignore the fact that these are elements and subsystems of organizations that are systems. Organizations have impact on individuals, and subsystems of individuals interact and place limits on each other (Schein, 1980; Schneider, 1976). The quality of training or the level of the compensation may put limits on the effectiveness and validity of the selection system and vice versa. Please keep that in mind as I cover each area.

Selection

A major area of research and application in I/O psychology has been selection. One of the earliest applications of psychology to this area was by Hugo Munsterberg in a study to select streetcar motormen in Boston in 1912 (Viteles, 1932). Since that time, thousands of studies on a wide variety of selection devices have been done. I find that students are either very skeptical or very impressed by the power of tests in assessing people and their ability to do jobs. I believe it is essential that we present what is known in a straightforward manner. Students should have some idea of the effectiveness or ineffectiveness of common selection devices that may someday open or close career opportunities for them. Not only is this an individual issue for students and psychologists, but there are also public policy questions involved that I'll come to later.

Many students have applied for and obtained jobs. I usually ask a few to describe the screening procedure they went through. Most went through some sort of interview. Through questioning, I usually find out that the session was fairly brief, that no guide was used by the interviewer, and that the interviewer did most of the talking and took no notes.

The research literature on the selection interview is very large, is composed of both field and laboratory studies, and is both correlational and experimental in nature. Generally speaking the results show that the interview is the most widely used selection device and is typically invalid. At least one reason for the lack of validity is the lack of a standardized interview guide; thus, comparisons among applicants are made on dissimilar data. My students get the point quickly when I ask one the sum of $2 + 2$ and another the square root of 3,763 and conclude that the second is worse in arithmetic.

Reviews by Hakel (1982), Schmitt (1976), and Carlson, Thayer, Mayfield, and Peterson (1971) offer leads to most of the studies in this area. Those interested in interpersonal perception and variables affecting impression formation will find a lot of valuable data in these studies, as dozens of variables have been studied that have an impact on the reliability and validity of interpersonal judgments. These studies are also of practical value if the interview is used in selecting students or new faculty. Schmitt, as his predecessor reviewers did, gives a number of suggestions that might be useful in interviewing. Some of these are

1. Using a structured interview guide to improve reliability
2. Taking notes and returning to them later to remove order effects and reduce the impact of negative information
3. Knowing the requirements of the job you're selecting for to help focus on relevant information
4. Training in ways to avoid bias effects such as leniency, halo, and so forth
5. Remembering that the interviewee is also forming impressions, thereby remembering the interviewer's public relations function
6. Letting the applicant talk so that an adequate behavior sample can be obtained, thereby avoiding a hasty decision.

I would add that letting the interviewee talk also helps one avoid leading the witness.

Many kinds of tests are used in selection. Those subjected to careful validation are clearly preferable to the interview. Generally speaking, however, I/O psychologists have less faith in tests than do their clinical and counseling brethren. There are lots of reasons for this, including the fact that equal employment opportunity (EEO) legislation and regulation insist on validity evidence in instances where protected groups—minorities, women, and so forth—score lower than majority groups (i.e., white males). Remember also the differences in response set for those applying for jobs versus those taking tests as part of a research project or coming to a counselor or therapist for help. Personality and interest measures are particularly vulnerable.

Testing for testing's sake is repugnant to many as an invasion of privacy. The use of tests in selection without demonstrated validity can also be costly to everyone. If the validity of any selection device is zero, people are rejected who have just as good a chance of performing well as those hired. There are many other societal costs that go along with using invalid devices. Tests or clinical interviews are not panaceas, but I will illustrate in a moment that some tests are better than they were once thought to be.

It is impossible to do justice to these data in the brief space I can allot here. Those interested should consult Dunnette (1976), Ghiselli (1966, 1973), and Grant (1980). Not surprisingly, ability and achievement tests have more consistent and higher validities for predicting training or job performance than personality and interest tests (Ghiselli, 1966, 1973).

For years, however, I/O psychologists have noted fluctuations in validity coefficients even for similar jobs in different places. We believed that company, task, work force, or other important differences caused these fluctuations, and therefore we held validity specificity as a major tenet of selection research (Guion, 1965). That is, we believed that one must validate a test locally to be sure it was appropriate for the job, even though it had been shown to predict performance for that job in many other places. As the federal government developed guidelines for using employment devices, it built in the concept of validity specificity. Indeed, it is a central theme of the Uniform Guidelines for Employee Selection Procedures (Equal Employment Opportunity Commission [EEOC], 1978), and is costing organizations many thousands of dollars to validate tests. Many are abandoning valid tests because of the expense and threat of suits and are relying on less valid and probably more biased methods, thinking to escape the guidelines. They will not, because the guidelines apply to anything used in a selection, placement, promotion, demotion, or discharge decision.

Also central to the Uniform Guidelines is the belief once held by many I/O psychologists that selection devices may have differential or single group validity for ethnic or other subgroups (Boehm, 1977; Katzell & Dyer, 1977). Bartlett, Bobbs, Mosier, and Hannan (1978) and Hunter, Schmidt, and Hunter (1979) present data that show that differential validity occurs only at the chance level. Although the argument goes on, evidence continues to mount not only that ability tests are valid across subgroups but also that they are fair in the sense that validity relationships appear to be the same. Differences in test scores for any group go with differences in job performance.

Of major importance, however, are the new meta-analytic procedures for integrating research from many studies, which have dealt a crippling blow to the concept of validity specificity. Schmidt and Hunter (1977; see also Hunter & Schmidt, 1982) developed a general solution to the problem and have to date produced over a dozen studies supporting the idea that validity generalization is the rule; specificity, if it exists, is the exception.

Returning to the main point, Schmidt, Hunter, and their colleagues have challenged a fundamental tenet of classic I/O psychology. They now state: "Professionally developed cognitive ability tests are valid predictors of performance on the job and in training for all jobs . . . in all settings" (Schmidt & Hunter, 1981, p. 1128). They appear to have carried the day as to validity generalization, even though others do not agree that validities are universal (Novick, 1982). They thus point to the importance of validity generalization in these days of concern over productivity: "The use of cognitive ability tests for selection in hiring can produce large labor cost savings, ranging from $18 million per year for small employers such as the Philadelphia police department (5,000 employees . . .) to $16 billion per year for large employers such as the federal government (4,000,000 employees . . .)" (Schmidt & Hunter, 1981, p. 1128). Unfortunately, the

low on consideration, for example, might be most effective; an office manager might, however, gain more effectiveness from consideration than from structuring. Despite some management training programs that stress both consideration and structuring, it became clear that the effectiveness of leader behavior depended on the situation.

Rather than my listing a host of references, I suggest reading Chemer's forthcoming chapter on leadership theory and research (in press). It gives a clear and concise review of much of the literature on leadership and an extensive bibliography and also does an excellent job of comparing various theories and placing them within a model that points to areas of integration and areas needing research and articulation. Although he is heavily identified with Fiedler's Contingency Model (Fiedler, Chemers, & Mahar, 1976), Chemers demonstrates a thorough and compassionate understanding of other approaches.

Briefly, he describes leader-oriented, transactional, and cognitive approaches to leadership. Fiedler's Contingency Model is the most thoroughly researched leader-oriented theory. Briefly put, whether a task-orientation (structuring) or relationship-orientation (consideration) is more effective depends on the leader's situational control. Control depends on leader-member relations, task structure, and the leader's position power. High control would result, for example, when a popular foreman with the power to hire and fire directed the activities of a group in a routine assembly task. Low control might characterize the situation of an elected leader of a social club; in that position power is weak and group goals and task structure may be nonexistent. The task-oriented leader is effective in high and low control settings. In the middle, where the leader may by dependent upon the expertise of individual members, serve at their pleasure, and have a moderately defined task—serving as head of a department of psychology, for example—a relationship-oriented leader may be more effective. Of course, such orientations are relative, and one can be both task- and relationship-oriented in one's behavior. This theory has been subjected to severe criticism, but a recent meta-analytic review offers strong support for it (Strube & Garcia, 1981).

I am stepping away from Chemer's review for a moment to point out that Fiedler believes that task or relationship orientation is a fundamental personality characteristic. Fiedler suggests that confronted with a situation that does not fit their leadership style, people change the situation to gain more or less control. Yes, people actually make the situation more difficult in some instances, so that the situation matches their leadership style.

Fiedler has become more flexible on this issue and accepts the possible effects of slight changes in leader behavior. He and his colleagues have developed a training program called Leader Match, however, which is designed to train leaders to change the situation to fit their styles rather than to change their behavior. Some of the controversy surrounding the contingency theory stems from this gloomy prospect of relative personal inflexibility.

Another leader-oriented theory is the Vroom and Yetton Normative Decision Model (Vroom & Yetton, 1974). This model focuses narrowly on one aspect of leadership—decision making. The model concerns itself with the importance of subordinate participation to commitment and motivation, as well as the importance of informational needs for a sound decision. The leader is concerned with making a high-quality decision and with acceptance of the decision by subordinates. If the leader needs information or help in solving the problem or commitment in implementing the decision, a participative decision-making style is indicated. If the solution is fairly clear and subordinate support exists, the leader can make a more autocratic decision. The leader balances informational and motivational needs against the time-consuming demands of participation. Vroom and Yetton believe the leader can adopt any decision-making style and provide a decision tree to help him or her choose feasible sets of decision styles. They even have a mechanical device to assist the leader in determining the feasible set of styles. Obviously, they believe leaders are more flexible than does Fiedler; the leader can make the decision and enforce it without consultation or may involve subordinates in many ways, even totally delegating authority for the decision and its implementation. Students have fun with the Vroom-Yetton model. If the Vroom and Yetton book is not readily available, there is enough information in Howell and Dipboye (1982, pp. 164–170) to work up class exercises. There is also an exercise outlined in Hall, Bowen, Lewicki, and Hall (1982, pp. 158–159).

The other leader-oriented theory reviewed is House's path-goal theory. In a concluding section, Chemers considers the similarities and differences among the three theories. Among these, he points out that the Fiedler and Vroom and Yetton models make similar predictions: task-oriented, directing behavior is most effective when the leader has high control or high certainty; considerate, relationship-oriented behavior is more appropriate when certainty or control is less. House seems to predict the opposite. But, as Chemers points out, Vroom and Yetton and Fiedler refer to the leader's uncertainty. House focuses on the follower's uncertainty. Thus, House would provide structure when the follower needs it and withhold it when the follower knows what to do. Consideration is provided instead.

Several other approaches are reviewed, with special emphasis on the threat of implicit leadership theories of subordinates to our research on leadership. Chemers concludes with a criticism and excellent illustrations of strengths and weaknesses of cross-cultural research and then proposes an integrative model. Chemer's chapter clearly shows how far we have come in leadership theory and research, and suggests how far and in what direction we have to go. A review of this literature may alert students to their own and their leaders' behavior, and it may even contribute to their effectiveness as leaders and followers. Having been at Ohio State in the early 1950s, I am impressed with how much more we know about leadership today. Simplistic models have been or are being rejected. I think we are very close to a good understanding of leadership. I am optimistic that our research will be better and that we will be able to improve the quality of leadership, both for greater effectiveness and greater follower satisfaction.

Motivation

Given the limits of this forum, I will shift the focus again to a related topic, motivation. As Locke and his colleagues (Locke, Shaw, Saari, & Latham, 1981) point out, traditional theories of motivation have not helped us much in understanding human behavior. I/O psychologists have, however, tried to apply various motivation theories and have developed several specific theories of work motivation—some need-based and some based on cognitive processes. Howell and Dipboye (1982) provide a good summary of the variety of theories used and developed by I/O psychologists, as well as some of the relevant research performed in organizations. As they point out, Maslow's seven-level hierarchy of needs has received little support and Alderfer (1972) has reduced the number of categories to three: existence, relatedness, and growth needs. However, Maslow's theory is still very popular with managers—and introductory text writers. So is Herzberg's two-factor theory of motivation (Herzberg, Mausner, & Snyderman, 1959), although support for it seems to be method bound (Dunnette, Campbell, & Hakel, 1967). I mention these two theories not because of their importance to I/O psychology today, but because students may encounter them on the job and probably should be forewarned of their lack of research support and utility. Herzberg contends that some job factors are hygienic and contribute to or prevent dissatisfaction. Other factors are motivators and contribute to performance and satisfaction. Obviously Herzberg's theory had enough truth in it to excite new research, and he should receive credit for that. However, he insists, for example, that pay is an hygienic factor and not a motivator, perpetuating the concept developed by the human relations movement that money is, at best, relatively unimportant. For those of us in the academic world, that may not be hard to believe—we are certainly not in this field for the big bucks. Money is, however, an important contributor to performance.

As I reviewed the treatment of motivation in several introductory textbooks, I was impressed by the concentration on biological motives and the brief treatment of motivational approaches to day-to-day human behavior. When the latter were discussed, social learning theory, attribution processes, and achievement motivation got a great deal of emphasis. Given the fact that many students will be working, it might be useful to look at work motivation theories. I have already indicated the major impact of social learning theory on training. McClelland's achievement motivation had only a brief day in the organizational sun and is treated by most I/O psychologists as an historical footnote.

Drowsier students may be excited by some of the more current approaches to work motivation. Not only is Locke's work on goal setting (Locke et al., 1981) significant for those concerned with human motivation and day-to-day behavior, but it also contains some important ideas that students could use in controlling and enhancing their own behavior. It might be worth a few minutes in class to highlight the Locke et al. review of the literature published in the *Psychological Bulletin* last year. Locke and his colleagues found overwhelming support for the efficacy of goal setting on performance, in both the laboratory and the field. Setting goals appears to direct attention and action, mobilize effort, prolong effort, and help develop appropriate strategies for goal attainment.

However, goal setting for some can be the equivalent of wishing. The same review by Locke et al. points out that specific, hard goals will result in higher achievement (ability held constant) than easy, "do-your-best," or no goals. Although not discussed in this review, it appears important to publicly commit to those goals, even though the evidence on commitment and acceptance is still muddy. Note that specific, quantitatively stated, hard goals improve performance better than those that are not.

Furthermore, feedback or knowledge of results relative to goal attainment appear to go hand in hand; they lose their effectiveness without each other. Thus, it is not enough to set a hard, specific goal; relevant measures of goal attainment must be ensured. If the job does not supply this, it should be restructured so that it will, or the goal should be stated in a different way. As an aside, let me make two personal, nonscientific observations. Students can help themselves on the job and can be helped in their courses by having goals made specific and challenging. If students have jobs where meaningful goals and feedbck are not available or possible, they may engage in activities that will yield feedback, even though the activities are relatively irrele vant to the organization's goals—self-defeating behavior.

For humanists, the effect of participation in goal setting on performance is unclear (Locke, Note 8). Recently, Locke speculated that participation probably had no impact on the motivational effect of goal setting. When participation did appear to affect productivity, it may have done so because clearer, more appropriate goals based on the knowledge of the participants had been set or because participants were involved in implementing the goals. The evidence is fairly clear, however, that glib comments about a "sense of ownership of the goal" having a motivating effect may be wrong. Goal acceptance depends on a host of variables, it seems, and participation's role is unclear. When participation does seem to affect performance, it appears to be the result of participation in the implementation of goal-directed activities rather than in the goal setting itself.

Some of these statements may rankle, seem counter-intuitive, or just seem wrong. I stress, however, that this summary reflects both laboratory and field studies and long-term as well as short-term effects. I am enthusiastic about laboratory research and the precision it yields. However, the human does not always operate in the short run. Long-term goals, rarely studied in the lab, can have powerful effects. More work on the impact of subgoals on performance would help us understand the effects of long and short term goals.

I'm sure that many psychologists know of job design experiments such as the Volvo experiment in which work teams build major components of a car. Many are probably familiar with job design concepts such as the sociotechnical systems of plant or job design, quality of work life, and job enlargement or enrichment. Most have heard reports that the use of quality circles in Japan has increased productivity levels over those of many U.S. industries. Although that last statement is not quite true—quality circles are not that common in Japan, may lose their effect quickly, and some of our industries, such as agribusiness, have much higher productivity rates than those in Japan—there is good reason to believe that job design can have motivational effects on both productivity and satisfaction.

For those interested in this area, I recommend *Work Redesign* by Hackman and Oldham (1980) for a quick review of different approaches to work motivation and a penetrating but readable exposition of their own theory. It is a "job characteristics" model that states that five basic job characteristics have strong psychological impact leading to high internal work motivation. If the job entails skill variety, task identity, and task significance, the psychological state achieved will be the experience of meaningful work. If the job provides autonomy, the individual experiences responsibility for work outcomes. If feedback is built into the job, that provides essential knowledge of results. Meaningfulness, responsibility, and knowledge of results then lead to high internal motivation, which is related to high growth satisfaction, high job satisfaction, and high work effectiveness. The following summarizes Hackman's (1980, pp. 449–450) description of relevant work:

1. Work redesign done properly increases satisfaction and motivation. It does not, however, increase satisfaction with organizational context such as pay, security, supervision, and so forth.

2. Quality of the product or service usually improves.

3. Quantity may go up, stay constant, or go down, depending upon preexisting conditions.

4. Effects on absenteeism and turnover are mixed.

Theories such as this one have called considerable attention to redesigning jobs so that tasks are combined to provide more variety, putting pieces of jobs disassembled on the assembly line back together to form meaningful or natural units, and pointing out how each person's job contributes to organizational goals. All these contribute primarily to meaningful work. "Vertical loading," or taking on functions formerly limited to higher levels, contributes to perceptions of autonomy, whereas feedback plays its traditional role. In many instances, there have been marked changes in behavior, performance, and satisfaction. Hackman and Oldham provide, however, for individual differences. Their theory provides for people with low growth needs and predicts that work redesign will not have salubrious effects for such people. At present, the theory has not gained overwhelming support. It is useful, however, as a technique for looking at jobs and work and more may be heard about it in the future.

There are many other theories in I/O psychology, including equity theory, Deci's cognitive evaluation theory, and a variety of valence-instrumentality-expectancy (VIE) theories—too many to review thoroughly here. Those I have covered seem to me more helpful to students at the moment. Other theories may ultimately carry the day, but they will have to incorporate many aspects of those theories described.

Before moving on, I must return, as promised, to money. Locke, Feren, McCaleb, Shaw, and Denny (Note 9) reviewed a sizable number of field studies of methods for motivating employee performance. Criteria for inclusion of a study in the review were rigorous. Incentive pay yielded the highest increase in employee performance on the average, followed by goal setting. Combining the two resulted in median performance improvements of 40%. Job enrichment followed in third place, with participation a very poor fourth with a median performance improvement of 0.5%. Now I am glad the role of incentive compensation and money has been rediscovered. The relationship between pay and performance is not simple, however. For rewards (pay) to motivate performance, several conditions must be present: "(1) important rewards can be given; (2) rewards can be varied depending on performance; (3) performance can be validly and inconclusively measured; (4) information can be provided that makes clear how rewards are given; (5) trust is high; and (6) employees accept the performance-based pay system" (Lawler, 1981, p. 100).

Each of these conditions seems important and, even if students are not intrigued by them, they might be useful in deciding how effective or ineffective pay systems are.

A related area that is creating a considerable stir in some segments of I/O psychology is behavior analysis. Depending on what you read, behavior analysis is a variant of behavior modification or a direct derivative of operant research. By focusing on behavioral contingencies, a number of I/O psychologists have developed new approaches to increasing productivity, reducing absenteeism and accidents, and improving maintenance (Babb & Kopp, 1978; Komaki, Collins, & Thoene, 1980). The approach has even been used to foster friendliness in fast food restaurants (Komaki, Blood, & Holder, 1980). The behavior analysis or behavior measurement approach focuses on specific aspects of job behavior that we often talk about but seem powerless to do much about. In the cited articles, Komaki and her colleagues developed operational measures of friendliness for fast food franchise employees and of tender loving care for nurses in a hospital. By arranging appropriate feedback and contingencies, they were able to improve these intangible but important aspects of behavior. Many other examples are available.

I believe that the application of behavior analytic techniques will become more widespread and that they will help us solve many seemingly intractable problems. Komaki et al., for example, refer to their efforts to improve preventive maintenance of equipment in the military. Think about it for a minute. Preventive maintenance is a low priority task. If it is not done, the vehicle may run anyway. If it is done, it is not always apparent and the boss may or may not give the worker credit. The only time the worker's performance becomes an issue is when the vehicle breaks down because preventive maintenance was not performed, perhaps by someone who was transferred to another duty station a year ago.

Believe it or not, Komaki and her colleagues developed a measurement and feedback approach to help solve this problem. The approach involves looking at jobs and behaviors in atypical ways—defining friendliness as smiling rather than grimacing—and providing simple ways to check on and reinforce the behavior. One thing that pleases me about the applications thus far is that they typically involve positive reinforcement rather than negative. Who knows, this kind of thinking could help us all. Maybe we could even figure out positive ways to get students to class on time—or even faculty to faculty meetings on time.

I do believe, however, that we should inject a note of caution in discussing these techniques. There are some commercial endeavors in this area that are clearly manipulative and simplistic. Putting a piece of gum on a machine every five minutes to reward workers can have a demeaning and counterproductive effect (Note 10). McDowell's (1982) paper on Herrnstein's restatement of the Law of Effect, for example, shows how complex the stimulus-response relationships are. Herrnstein's restatement indicates that the response rate depends on both the reinforcement rate for responding *and* the extraneous reinforcement present in the environment. Thus use of behavior modification techniques requires a high level of sophistication. It should also require high ethical standards. We and students should be forewarned to look carefully at simple solutions to complex behavioral problems.

Job Satisfaction

A variable related to motivation is job satisfaction, an issue that will also be of interest to your students someday. We have come a long way from the naive view of the human relations school that satisfaction causes good performance. Satisfaction and job performance are often uncorrelated, a fact that will not surprise those of you who have struggled with the attitude-behavior relationship in social psychology. When a relationship exists, there are those who believe that performance causes job satisfaction. If I am doing well on the job, I am more satisfied than if I am not. It is a messy picture, and I suspect we will be working a long time with our social psychologist colleagues in understanding the attitude-behavior relationship (Steers & Porter, 1979).

It has been alleged that job satisfaction among workers has been going to hell in a handbasket. Indeed, there has been evidence in national surveys of declines in worker satisfaction. Developmental psychologists sensitive to cohort effects will appreciate how sensitive such indices can be. When one partials out age mix—and young workers are typically more negative—there is no evidence of decline. Unfortunately, people pick data they want without proper analysis. I doubt that job satisfaction in the American work force is going down (Kanter, 1982).

I should point out that there are some I/O psychologists who believe that job satisfaction is a separate and legitimate goal in and of itself, regardless of its relationship to performance (Nord, 1977). I lean in this direction myself, and there are many industrial decision makers who agree. Certainly the whole Quality of Work Life movement is a strong component of this sort of thinking, although there is often a component of enlightened self-interest, too. Job dissatisfaction often has undesirable side effects such as absenteeism, turnover, restriction of output, and grievances, which one would like to avoid. I emphasize that I believe both employer and employee want to avoid these side effects.

I/O Psychology and Unions

On the subject of I/O psychology and unions, I must acknowledge that I/O psychology has been accused of having a strong management or organizational bias. It would be hard to deny that the organization controls access to research sites, provides compensation for services, and so forth. Relatively few I/O psychologists have become involved in work with and publication about psychology and unions. Ross Stagner and R. J. Kornhauser were post-World War II pioneers (Rosen & Stagner, 1980). More recently, Jeanne Brett (1980), Neal Schmitt (1979), and Michael Gordon (Gordon & Nurick, 1981) have been quite active.

As Rosen and Stagner point out, unions have doubted our impartiality. In addition, secrecy is often seen by the union as essential to the collective bargaining process. Some striking changes are taking place, however, as organizations such as GM and the UAW work together on Quality of Work Life programs. I/O psychologists have been heavily involved in such efforts.

Division 14 has made a commitment to encourage I/O-union endeavors and to aid in disseminating the findings (Gordon & Nurick, 1981). Gordon, Philpot, Burt, Thompson, and Spiller (1980) have developed an instrument for measuring union commitment. Those who are interested in this topic might want to read the Gordon and Nurick paper for a quick overview of recent developments. I/O psychologists are having an impact. The National Labor Relations Board, for example, used psychological research to resolve a charge of unfair collective bargaining. Gordon and Nurick also list several examples of research of potential interest to I/O and social psychologists.

Conclusion

I am sure that I have disappointed a number of my colleagues because I have omitted their favorite topic or have highlighted one they think merits less or no attention. I have ignored much of traditional I/O psychology, including some of my pets, and completely skipped consumer and engineering psychology. I hope both of those areas will be represented in the G. Stanley Hall Lecture Series in future years.

A major consideration in my selections has been the interests of introductory psychology students as I have seen them. Students are interested in the application of psychology to many settings. They belong to organizations and will one day probably join the world of work. I have tried to tell you so that you can tell them some of the things we know of that world in the order they might experience them: from the selection process, through organizational entry, to the impact of challenging assignments, and individual development and training. I have tried to tell you what we know about leaders and leadership that will affect them, and some of what we know about motivation and job satisfaction. Finally, I indulged my own interest in unions. I have had to treat each area separately, even though these interact and impose limits on or enhance effects. A change in any subsystem—selection, training, compensation, job design, leadership—reverberates throughout every other subsystem. That is one of the challenges of doing research in and applying our knowledge of I/O psychology.

Reference Notes

1. Kalat, J. W. Personal communication, November 1981.
2. Howard, A. *Who are the industrial/organizational psychologists?* APA Division 14, January 1982, p. 24.
3. APA Division 14, *Guidelines for Doctoral Level Training in I/O Psychology,* 1982.
4. Horner, S. D., Mobley, W. H., & Meglino, B. M. *An experimental evaluation of the effects of a realistic job preview on marine recruit affect, interactions, and behavior.* Columbia, SC Center for Mangement and Organizational Research, University of South Carolina Technical Report-9, 1979.
5. Hollmann, T. D., & Hollenback, J. H. *Early career development of entry level professionals.* General Electric Corporate Employment Relations Operation, December 1979.
6. Howard, A. *Managerial lives in transition: Advancing age and changing times.* Southeastern Psychological Association, Atlanta, GA, March 1981.
7. Chemers, M. *Leadership.* Office of Naval Research Conference on Productivity, Nags Head, NC, June 1982.
8. Locke, E. A. *Eighteen years of research on goal setting.* Office of Naval Research Conference on Productivity: Nags Head, NC, June 1982.
9. Locke, E. A., Feren, D. B., McCaleb, V. M., Shaw, K. N., & Denny, A. T. *The relative effectiveness of four methods of motivating employee performance.* American Psychological Association, New York, September 1979.
10. McGehee, W. Personal communication, July 1982.

References

Alderfer, C. P. *Existence, relatedness and growth: Human needs in organizational settings.* New York: Free Press, 1972.

Babb, H. W., & Kopp, D. G. Applications of behavior modification in organizations: A review and critique. *Academy of Management Review,* 1978, *3,* 281–292.

Bales, R. F., & Slater, P. E. Role differential in small decision-making groups. In T. Parsons & R. F. Bales (Eds.), *Family socialization and interaction processes.* New York: Free Press, 1955.

Bandura, A. *Social learning theory.* Englewood Cliffs, NJ: Prentice-Hall, 1977.

Bartlett, C. J., Bobbs, P., Mosier, S. B., & Hannan, R. Testing for fairness with a moderated regression strategy: An alternative to differential analysis. *Personnel Psychology,* 1978, *31,* 233–241.

Boehm, V. R. Differential prediction: A methodological artifact? *Journal of Applied Psychology,* 1977, *62,* 146–154.

Bray, D. W., Campbell, R. J., & Grant, D. L. *The management recruit: Formative years in business.* New York: Wiley-Interscience, 1973.

Brett, J. M. Behavioral research on unions and union management systems. In B. M. Staw & L. L. Cummings (Eds.), *Research in organizational behavior* (Vol. 2). Greenwich, CT: Jai Press, 1980.

Carlson, R. E., Thayer, P. W., Mayfield, E. C., & Peterson, D. A. Improvements in the selection interview. *Personnel Journal,* 1971, *50,* 268–275.

Chemers, M. M. Leadership theory and research: A systems-process integration. In P. B. Paulus (Ed.), *Basic group processes.* New York: Springer-Verlag, in press.

Decker, P. J. The enhancement of behavior modeling training of supervisory skills by the inclusion of retention processes. *Personnel Psychology,* 1982, *35,* 323–332.

Dunnette, M. D. (Ed.). *Handbook of industrial and organizational psychology.* Chicago: Rand McNally, 1976.

Dunnette, M. D., Campbell, J. P., & Hakel, M. D. Factors contributing to job satisfaction and job dissatisfaction in six occupational groups. *Organizational Behavior & Human Performance,* 1967, *2,* 143–174.

Equal Employment Opportunity Commission, Department of Labor, & Department of Justice. Uniform guidelines for employee selection procedures. *Federal Register,* 1978, *43,* 38290–39315.

Fiedler, F. E., Chemers, M. M., & Mahar, L. *Improving leader effectiveness: The leader match concept.* New York: Wiley, 1976.

Ghiselli, E. E. *The validity of occupational aptitude tests.* New York: Wiley, 1966.

Ghiselli, E. E. The validity of aptitude tests in personnel selection. *Personnel Psychology,* 1973, *26,* 461–477.

Goldstein, A. P., & Sorcher, M. *Changing supervisor behavior.* New York: Pergamon Press, 1974.

Goldstein, I. L. Training in work organizations. *Annual Review of Psychology,* 1980, *31,* 229–272.

Goldstein, I. L., & Buxton, V. M. Training in human performance. In E. A. Fleishman & M. D. Dunnette (Eds.), *Human performance and productivity: Vol. 1. Human capability assessment.* Hillsdale, NJ: Erlbaum, 1982.

Gordon, M. E., & Nurick, A. J. Psychological approaches to the study of unions and union-management relations. *Psychological Bulletin,* 1981, *90,* 293–306.

Gordon, M. E., Philpot, J, W., Burt, R, E., Thompson, C, E., & Spiller, W. E. Commitment to the union: Development of a measure and an examination of its correlates [Monograph]. *Journal of Applied Psychology,* 1980, *65,* 479–499.

Grant, D. L. Issues in personnel selection. *Professional Psychology,* 1980, *11,* 369–384.

Guion, R. M. *Personnel testing.* New York: McGraw-Hill, 1965.

Hackman, J. R., & Oldman, G. R. *Work redesign.* Reading, MA: Addison-Wesley, 1980.

Hakel, M. D. Employment interviewing. In K. M. Rowland & G. R. Ferris (Eds.), *Personnel management.* Boston: Allyn & Bacon, 1982.

Hall, D. T., Bowen, D. D., Lewicki, R. J., & Hall, F. S. *Experiences in management and organizational behavior.* New York: Wiley, 1982.

Herzberg, F., Mausner, B., & Snyderman, B. *The motivation to work.* New York: Wiley, 1959.

Howell, W. C., & Dipboye, R. L. *Essentials of industrial and organizational psychology* (rev. ed.). Homewood, IL: Dorsey Press, 1982.

Hunter, J. E., & Schmidt, F. L. Fitting people to jobs: The impact of personnel selection on national productivity. In M. D. Dunnette & E. A. Fleishman (Eds.), *Human performance and productivity: Human capability assessment* (Vol.1). Hillsdale, NJ: Erlbaum, 1982.

Hunter, J. E., Schmidt, F. L., & Hunter, R. Differential validity of employment tests by race: A comprehensive review and analysis. *Psychological Bulletin,* 1979, *86,* 721–735.

Kanter, R. M. Work in a new America. *Daedalus,* 1982, *107,* 47–78.

Katzell, R. A., & Dyer, F. J. Differential validity reviewed. *Journal of Applied Psychology*, 1977, *62*, 137–145.

Knowlton, W. A., Jr., & Mitchell, T. R. The effects of causal attributions on supervisors' evaluations of subordinate performance. *Journal of Applied Psychology*, 1980, *65*, 459–466.

Komaki, J., Blood, M. R., & Holder, D. Fostering friendliness in a fast food franchise. *Journal of Organizational Behavior Management*, 1980, *2*, 151–163.

Komaki, J., Collins, R. L., & Theone, T. J. F. Behavioral measurement in business, industry and government. *Behavioral Assessment*, 1980, *2*, 103–123.

Lawler, E. E. *Pay and organizational development.* Reading, MA: Addison-Wesley, 1981.

Locke, E. A., Shaw, K. N., Saari, L. M., & Latham, G. P. Goal-setting and task performance: 1969–1980. *Psychological Bulletin*, 1981, *90*, 125–152.

McDowell, J. J. The importance of Herrnstein's mathematical statement of the law of effect. *American Psychologist*, 1982, *37*, 771–779.

McGehee, W., & Tullar, W. L. A note on evaluating behavior modification and behavior modeling as industrial training techniques. *Personnel Psychology*, 1978, *31*, 477–484.

Nord, W. R. Job satisfaction reconsidered. *American Psychologist*, 1977, *32*, 1026–1035.

Novick, M. R. Report on test standards revision. *The Industrial-Organizational Psychologist*, 1982, *19*, 10–12.

Rosen, H., & Stagner, R. Industrial/organizational psychology and unions: A viable relationship? *Professional Psychology*, 1980, *11*, 477–483.

Schein, E. H. *Organizational psychology* (3rd ed.). Englewood Cliffs, NJ: Prentice-Hall, 1980.

Schmidt, F. L., & Hunter, J. E. Development of a general solution to the problem of validity generalization. *Journal of Applied Psychology*, 1977, *62*, 529–540.

Schmidt, F. L., & Hunter, J. E. Employment testing: Old theories and new research findings. *American Psychologist*, 1981, *36*, 1128–1137.

Schmitt, N. Union-psychologist cooperative efforts. *The Industrial-Organizational Psychologist*, 1979, *16*, 31–32.

Schmitt, N. Social and situational determinants of interview decisions: Implications for the employment interview. *Personnel Psychology*, 1976, *29*, 79–101.

Schneider, B. H. *Staffing organizations.* Pacific Palisades, CA: Goodyear, 1976.

Sorcher, M., & Spence, R. The interface project: Behavior modeling as social technology in South Africa. *Personnel Psychology*, 1982, *35*, 557–582.

Steers, R. M., & Porter, L. W. *Motivation and work behavior* (2nd ed.). New York: McGraw-Hill, 1979.

Stogdill, R. M. Personal factors associated with leadership: A survey of the literature. *Journal of Psychology*, 1948, *25*, 35–71.

Strube, M. J., & Garcia, J. E. A meta-analytic investigation of Fiedler's contingency model of leadership effectiveness. *Psychological Bulletin*, 1981, *90*, 307–321.

Viteles, N. S. *Industrial psychology.* New York: Norton, 1932.

Vroom, V. H., & Yetton, P. *Leadership and decision making.* Pittsburgh: University of Pittsburgh Press, 1974.

Wanous, J. P. Organizational entry: Newcomers moving from outside to inside. *Psychological Bulletin*, 1977, *84*, 601–618.

COMMENTS

A s Paul Thayer observes early in his lecture, most students taking an introductory psychology course have had the experience of applying for and obtaining a job. The world of work is already assuming the place of importance it will retain throughout most of their lives. Despite this, Thayer's informal survey revealed that introductory texts typically dedicate only two sentences to industrial/organizational (I/O) psychology. Moreover, it appears that many introductory courses are taught by experimental or social psychologists whose own knowledge of I/O psychology may be equally as limited.

Another factor that may have discouraged thorough coverage of I/O psychology in introductory courses is the "multiplicity of our activities, our backgrounds, and the places where we work." Because I/O psychology touches on so many different areas, it is next to impossible to cover all these in any depth. But the common theme throughout the field is "our concern with research and application in the world of work."

Several questions during the discussion following Thayer's presentation cast additional light on points made during the lecture.

Question. Dr. Thayer, where would you include a discussion of I/O psychology in the introductory psychology course?

Answer. I think that my colleague from North Carolina State University, Professor Jim Kalat, could best answer that question because he has been doing that sort of thing. (Kalat then suggested that a complete presentation of I/O psychology might logically follow the introductory course section on social psychology.) Training should logically follow the material on learning; selection would appropriately follow a discussion of individual differences; and interviewing might well be presented after therapeutic interviews and related matters such as counseling, the applications of clinical skills, interviewing, and the like.

Question. In discussing Locke's work, you seem to accept the idea of a relationship between participation and motivation, and, therefore, the idea that employee participation should be played down.

Answer. That is not what I intended to say. What I meant to say is that Locke's work seems to indicate that the participant's role does not have a motivating effect. Where it does have an effect, it seems to be because participation helps define goals or because of the individual's unique knowledge or because individuals who have participated understand the situation better and so are better able to implement those goals. But this also suggests that the effect of participation is not to motivate.

Question. Do you think managers should emphasize their subordinates' job satisfaction?

Answer. My own particular view is that it is very important for an individual to get some kind of satisfaction out of his or her daily activities, and I agree with Walter Nord that this is a legitimate end in and of itself, regardless of its relationship to productivity or absenteeism or anything else.

Question. How do you view participation?

Answer. Whether participation is helpful or not depends on various factors. I think a contingency model is as important for participation as for leadership. This is exactly what the Vroom model says. Think about it for a moment. Suppose your department head involved you in every decision. You would want to say, "For Pete's sake, what are you here for? You make the minor decisions and only involve me in the important ones." Participation in everything is probably bad news. If the decision directly affects me, I will want to be involved. But if the decision is whether to buy two reams of paper, my office manager should take care of it and not bother me.

FLORENCE L. DENMARK

INTEGRATING THE PSYCHOLOGY OF WOMEN INTO INTRODUCTORY PSYCHOLOGY

Florence L. Denmark is a professor of psychology at Hunter College and the Graduate School of the City University of New York (CUNY). Prior to her election to the presidency of the American Psychological Association (APA) in 1980, she had served as the executive officer of the doctoral program in psychology at CUNY. Denmark is a fellow of APA and is a former national president of both Psi Chi and of the Division of the Psychology of Women of APA. She has served on the Board of Governors of the New York Academy of Sciences and on the Board of Directors of the Eastern Psychological Association. She is a past president of the New York State Psychological Association. Denmark is currently chair of APA's Committee on Women and a member of its Committee on International Relations in Psychology.

Denmark is the editor of *Women: A PDI Research Reference Work, Volume 1* and coeditor of *Woman: Dependent or Independent Variable?* and *The Psychology of Women: Future Directions in Research.* Denmark has coauthored a forthcoming book, *Women's Realities; Women's Choices.* She has also been honored as a Mellon Scholar at St. Olaf College and with an Outstanding Woman in Science Award by the Association for Women in Science. Denmark received her doctorate from the University of Pennsylvania. She has published extensively in the field of social psychology. As a renowned authority in the field of psychology of women, Denmark has frequently taken part in symposiums and has, by invitation, delivered major addresses before scientific and professional audiences.

FLORENCE L. DENMARK

INTEGRATING THE PSYCHOLOGY OF WOMEN INTO INTRODUCTORY PSYCHOLOGY

I will begin by making some observations. The first concerns G. Stanley Hall, the father of child psychology and the first president of the American Psychological Association (APA); the second concerns an informal analysis of the current textbook situation; and the third concerns the importance of mainstreaming information on the psychology of women into topics covered in introductory psychology courses. Most of this essay concerns this last topic.

I would like to call your attention to four women who have made significant contributions to psychology, the psychology of women, and the history of psychology. All four died, in their prime, during the 1981–82 academic year. It is to these women I dedicate this essay: Clara Mayo, past president of the Society for the Psychological Study of Social Issues; Jeanne Block, a noted developmental psychologist; Barbara Dohrenwend, a renowned epidemiologist; and Carolyn Sherif, a former president of Division 35, a G. Stanley Hall lecturer, and a feminist researcher. Each woman enhanced psychology with brilliant research and skill as a theoretist. Their contributions and personal insights will be missed.

I also want to thank the following people who served as my sounding board when I was planning this paper and who provided me with valuable resource information. They are Frances Francois, Laurel Furumoto, Sandra Gonsalves, Cheryl Harding, Nancy Russo, Gwen Stevens, Rhoda Unger, Mary Roth Walsh, and Christina Taylor. Ronna Kabatznick, my graduate assistant, provided invaluable research and editorial assistance.

G. Stanley Hall

It is ironic that a paper on the psychology of women should be given in honor of one of the most vocal anti-feminists[1] psychology has ever known. G. Stanley Hall's attitudes toward women were so negative and degrading that it is surprising that he is held in such high regard. In a talk he gave against coeducation at the American Academy of Medicine in 1906, Hall remarked:

> It [coeducation] violates a custom so universal that it seems to express a fundamental human instinct. . . . girls . . . are attracted to common knowledge which all share, to the conventional, are more influenced by fashions, more imitative and lack the boy's intense desire to know, be, do something distinctive that develops and emphasizes his individuality. To be thrown on their own personal resources in sports, in the classroom, in nature study and elementary laboratory brings out the best in a boy, but either confuses or strains a girl. (pp. 1–2)

If these remarks are not enough, he goes on to say that

> equal pay to the teachers of boys and girls is unfair. . . . Good teachers of boys should be paid more. . . . Sex distinctions should at this age be pushed to their utmost. Boys should be more masculine and girls more feminine. (p. 3)

Hall actively discriminated against women and urged others to do so as well. Mary Roth Walsh reported in her book, *Doctors Wanted: No Women Need Apply* (1977, p. 204), that in a commencement speech given at the College of Physicians and Surgeons in Boston in 1908, Hall ridiculed aspiring women doctors and suggested that they stay clear of medicine because of their penchant for hysteria and their menstrual difficulties.

M. Carey Thomas, an active feminist and president of Bryn Mawr College from 1894 through 1922, openly renounced Hall's antagonistic attacks on women:

> I had never chanced again upon a book that seemed to me to degrade me in my womanhood as the seventh and seventeenth chapters on women and women's education of President G. Stanley Hall's *Adolescence*. (Thomas, 1908, p. 65)

---

[1]A feminist is someone who favors political, social, and economic equality of women and men, and therefore favors the social and legal changes necessary to achieve that equality.

Although G. Stanley Hall's attitudes and remarks about women's psychology appear extreme and ridiculous today, it cannot be forgotten that his views appeared in the first and most widely read textbook on child and adolescent psychology. It can be safely assumed that his personal beliefs influenced hundreds of teachers and students. Today it is unlikely that either a textbook author or a former president of the APA would explicitly state such derogatory remarks about women. During the past ten years, the psychology of women has received the serious attention of scholars and scientists, and, as a result, many people have become intolerant of untested and sexist beliefs and opinions.

Nevertheless, introductory textbooks do communicate anti-female attitudes. The sexism is subtle and therefore tends to be more insidious and persistent than the type of sexism that can easily be identified. This leads us to my second topic: An analysis of the current textbook situation.

The Current Textbook Situation

Prior to writing this paper, in order to find out exactly how women are portrayed in introductory psychology books, I conducted an informal study. The purpose of the study was to examine how and if authors integrated up-to-date material on the psychology of women, to see whether feminist analyses and critiques were included, and to see how photographs and examples portrayed women.

I first asked a number of undergraduate majors in psychology at Hunter College, where I teach, whether or not their course in introductory psychology included material related to the psychology of women. Most of them said it did not, and a few indicated that only minimal attention was given to women's issues.

I then sampled 16 introductory textbooks published between 1979 and 1982.[2] I expected that these textbooks would not have incorporated the new research on women and that those that did would give only cursory attention to this material. This was true for the 1979 and 1980 textbooks. However, my assumption was incorrect for the books published in 1981 and 1982. These more recent books, however, did not give what I would consider excellent coverage of the psychology of women. In general the topics about women were unevenly covered. Some texts included many topics whereas others covered only one or two. As Jane Ewens Holbrook illustrated (Note 1), these topics frequently seemed to be tacked on as an afterthought.

[2]There were 129 introductory psychology textbooks available as of 1982, compared to 98 in 1981 (Rogers & Magan, 1982).

The topics and issues included sex-role development, sex-role stereo-types, achievement motivation, prejudice against women, sex differences in personality, and sexual development, which sometimes included lesbianism. Occasionally textbooks critiqued topics such as sociobiology and psychoanalysis from a feminist perspective, but more often they did not.

Let me note that merely including information on the psychology of women does not mean that this treatment is adequate or fair. For example, anorexia nervosa, a prevalent eating disorder among women, is rarely mentioned and when it is, there is little discussion about certain oppressive and conflicting social forces that are thought to influence the onset of the illness.

One area covered extensively is female and male sexuality. But many of the studies cited about women's sexuality had already been superseded by newer research. Rarely does a discussion of women's orgasmic capacity—which far exceeds that of males during sexual intercourse—figure prominently in these sections. And I must say, I have yet to receive an adequate explanation as to why rape is always included in the sexual behavior sections and never in chapters on aggression or social deviance.

Additional bias in textbook coverage of feminist material is found in the research selected for attention and discussion. For instance, Karen Horney's (1939) and Clara Thompson's (1964) theoretical work on female psychology, which contradicted Freud's thinking, is cited in only one text. But Matina Horner's study on women's fear of success (1972) appeared in most of the books. I am afraid that it has become standard practice to present largely pessimistic views of women.

In the final analysis, the textbooks do state, in words, that there is no firm evidence to justify extensive sex differences. But the illustrations and examples used throughout the books point to a different conclusion. Women are presented to students through photographs as phobic, anxious, emotional, and mentally ill. The female character from *Three Faces of Eve* is used to illustrate multiple personality disorders whereas the fictional character of Dr. Jekyll and Mr. Hyde is ignored. Similarly, Lady MacBeth is used to illustrate obsessive-compulsive behavior, but never is Dostoyevski's Roshkolnikov used. Joan of Arc experiences hallucinations, but the male biblical characters who also heard voices are completely ignored. Females are more frequently depicted as overweight, as mental patients, or as watching males conduct scientific experiments. Males, on the other hand, solve complex mathematical problems and are more often seen in the role of experimenter or psychotherapist. The significant psychologists pictured in the textbooks are most frequently male; rarely is a female psychologist featured. Thus women continue to be depicted as sick or passive whereas men are depicted as intellectual, healthy, and strong. This bias in the selection of illustrative material that reinforces the culturally accepted female/male stereotype cannot be blamed on one or two texts. It was found throughout most of the books reviewed.

If there is any doubt that these considerations are important, never forget that the credibility and prestige of the source—the basic introductory text—is a powerful influence on the naïve reader.

The quality of the texts I reviewed in terms of their feminist content was very disappointing. The textbooks were extremely homogeneous, giving strikingly similar coverage to similar topics. One wonders how much the texts are copied from each other and why they are not creative and interesting.

I must note one 1982 textbook by Louis Janda and Karen Klenke-Hamel that is an exceptionally good book. Although it does not include more recent material on the psychology of women, it is unbiased and feminist in its approach. The title of the book is *Psychology: Its Study and Uses*.

Mainstreaming the Psychology of Women Into the Introductory Course

The questions writers of introductory textbooks must address are whether to include and where to place material relating to women, sex differences, and sex roles. The most popular but least acceptable decision has been to include only a negligible amount of information in a few chapters. When authors do include this information, as they should, is it more useful to relegate this material to a separate chapter or should it be mainstreamed throughout the textbook? I do not think it should be an either/or situation. We should both mainstream and have a separate chapter on the psychology of women. I will explain this reasoning.

The relevance of the study of the psychology of women is not always obvious to instructors. If the text does not incorporate this material throughout the book, instructors frequently will not find out what the issues are or read up on the relevant literature and then select the appropriate material to integrate into their courses.

On the other hand, if the psychology of women material is in a separate chapter, it is too easy for the instructor to ignore and exclude it. As an instructor of introductory psychology, I know how easy it is to omit several chapters of a text, many times through necessity. This practice is even more common in introductory courses that meet over one instead of two semesters. Consequently, if the psychology of women material is segregated into one chapter, I can guess with certainty at least one chapter that will be omitted by many instructors. If, however, the material is mainstreamed, instructors would be obliged to teach topics in the psychology of women as they teach the biological foundations of behavior, human development, motivation, personality, and psychotherapy—to name just a few areas. Moreover, if authors merely place a special unit on the psychology of women at the end of the textbook or course, this may give students the erroneous impression that women are important only as an afterthought or as a supplementary gesture. I believe that it would be more valuable and responsible to transform the entire introductory course to include scholarship on women. This should be done with seriousness and considerable skill. It is time for traditional course materials to be replaced with newer and more egalitarian materials.

I believe the best solution is to mainstream the psychology of women material whenever and wherever relevant throughout the course. In addition, I believe it is essential to have a chapter that exclusively highlights additional scholarship and research in the psychology of women. The latter would offer an opportunity for the instructor and the student to obtain a deeper and richer understanding of the field.

This essay focuses on issues that fit into some of the mainstream topics usually taught in introductory courses. (I will leave it to the writers of introductory texts to determine which aspects of the psychology of women should be put into a separate chapter.) I will focus on these six issues:

1. The Women of Psychology
2. Methodological Issues
3. Moral Development From a Feminist Perspective
4. Biological Foundations of Behavior and Sex Differences
5. Personality and Mental Health Issues
6. Women and Social Behavior.

Every issue relevant to women cannot be developed here. I have selected topics that I feel should be included in an introductory course but that are either ignored or given biased coverage. Sexuality, including physical development, hetero/homosexuality, sexual dysfunction, or other sexual issues will not be discussed here. Neither will pregnancy, menstruation, menopause, or sex-role development. Stereotyping, prejudice, physical attractiveness, aggression, achievement, and women and work will also be omitted. Some of these topics are already given adequate coverage in introductory texts. However, for those who want in-depth and feminist coverage in these topics, refer to the Suggested Reading list on page 61 for selected books and articles that provide an overview of the psychology of women.

The Women of Psychology

A survey by Cox et al. (1982) indicated that one third of the respondents took a course in general psychology for the purpose of understanding and improving themselves as well as understanding and dealing with others. This implies that students—females and males—want information about both women and men. To accomplish this, introductory courses must acknowledge women and their contributions to psychology.

It is my belief that a statement should be made in the beginning of each course on introductory psychology—a statement that says that not everyone in the history of psychology is male. Many very outstanding psychologists were women.

One sure way to make students aware of women's contributions to the history of psychology is to highlight the first names of theorists and researchers (Russo & Malovich, 1982). It should be made clear that many well-known names in psychology belong to both female and male contributors. Too frequently names such as Clark, Hilgard, Lacey, Murphy, Sears, and Spence are associated with their male identities rather than their female identities (see Denmark, 1980). How many students—and psychologists—realize that test names often reflect their female innovators: names such as "Loretta" Bender, "Psyche" Cattell, "Maud" Merrill, and "Florence" Goodenough, to mention only a few (Denmark, 1980)?

Are students aware of the achievements of the women presidents of the APA? Mary Calkins; Margaret Washburn; Anne Anastasi; Leona Tyler; president-elect, Janet Taylor Spence; and I are all significant contributors to the history of psychology.

Mary Calkins was more than a student of William James as she has been described by Watson (1971). She was the inventor of the paired-associate technique, founder of an early psychology laboratory at Wellesley College, and the creator of a system of self-psychology.

Margaret Floy Washburn was the first woman to receive a PhD in psychology. She built the psychology laboratory at Vassar College and was the author of a very significant text in comparative psychology, *The Animal Mind.*

While examining the first edition of *American Men of Science*, published by James NcKeen Cattell in 1906, Laurel Furumoto (Note 2) identified 22 women psychologists. These women compose approximately 12% of the total number of psychologists in the volume. Furumoto points out that, although these women were in many ways comparable to their male counterparts, their career paths differed. Many of the women's careers were characterized by frequent job changes, gaps in employment, and little evidence of professional advancement. This was particularly true for married women. Those who did advance through the academic ranks were single and employed typically at women's colleges. Marriage and career were mutually exclusive. Although the value of coeducation versus single-sex education for women has been questioned, it is clear that women's colleges were providing a unique opportunity for women to serve on the faculty.

For those with a strong interest in the history of women in psychology, I recommend Gwendolyn Stevens and Sheldon Gardner's two-volume work, *The Women of Psychology* (1982) and Agnes O'Connell and Nancy Russo's book, *Models of Achievement: Reflections of Eminent Women in Psychology* (1983). Russo and O'Connell have also published "Models From Our Past: Psychology's Foremothers" (1980). Furumoto presented a paper, "Women in American Psychology: An Attempt To Reconstruct the Experience of the First Generation (1890–1920)," at the 1982 Eastern Psychological Association Conference. I will be happy to provide copies of my 1980 APA Presidential Address, "Psyche: From Rocking the Cradle to Rocking the Boat," which also contains historical material, upon request. Psychology appears to be a different discipline when it is seen through the eyes of its women contributors.

Methodological Issues

Most introductory courses include sections on research methodology. Various research paradigms are considered and, of course, throughout the course illustrations of studies are presented both in the text and in the lecture. A teacher of introductory psychology should be aware of the ways in which sex bias may affect the research cited in introductory texts and presented in the classroom lectures.

The investigator may begin with a biased theoretical model such as Freud's psychoanalytic theory or Wilson's sociobiology. It is important to be aware of the stated or inferred orientation of the researcher.

Sex-role stereotypes have also influenced the questions that are asked and the interpretation of results. Thus studies are frequently carried out on women's mood changes as related to their monthly menstrual cycles. But why not ask whether men also experience cyclical mood fluctuations?

If women and men differ in results on a test of field dependence such as the Embedded Figures Test (EFT) or the rod-and-frame test (RFT), this is usually interpreted to mean that men and women have different cognitive styles—men are more "field independent," more analytical, and possibly more independent than are women. One could have concluded that women are more field sensitive, more perceptive in terms of their environment, or even that these differences are simply ones of visual perception. Eleanor Maccoby (1969, pp. 68–98) found females just as capable as males of detecting stimuli in an auditory context. Herman Witken and his colleagues (1968) found no sex differences when the EFT was presented in a tactile concept.

Studies of Eskimos failed to find sex differences even in visual spatial tasks (Berry, 1966). This finding points out the importance of looking at the cultural context in which research is carried out. Eskimo children of both sexes are granted considerable independence. Other researchers have indicated the importance of learning and practice on visual-spatial ability (e.g., Sherman, 1967, 1974).

Bias also exists in the selection of subjects for psychological research. In addition to the overuse of introductory psychology students in research, males are used much more frequently than are females. As Hyde and Rosenberg pointed out (1980), this is true for animal research as well as for human research. For example, Wendy McKenna and Suzanne Kessler (1977) surveyed social-psychological research on aggression in humans. They found that approximately 50% of all research used male subjects only, 10% used females only, and only 40% used both males and females.

When Suzanne Prescott (1978) asked a group of 67 researchers why they used single-sex designs, the answers they received included "scientific" reasons such as "we don't want to study known differences," and practical reasons such as the availability of subjects. They also received "extrascientific" answers such as not being able to bring oneself to manipulate the anxiety associated with college girls. Such reasons certainly do not permit sex-fair research.

An experiment may also yield different results depending on whether the experimenter is male or female. Remember that the majority of psychological research has also been conducted by men. Of course, expectations of observers can influence what they see. Thus, observers of infants reported the behavior of a child differently depending on whether they were told the child was a boy or a girl (e.g., Sidorowicz & Lunney, 1980) even though the child observed was the same one.

Perhaps the biggest problem one finds is the assumption underlying much of the research that sex differences exist and that these differences are important. Much of the data reflecting differences is exaggerated. Even where differences are found, the intra-sex differences are much greater than the differences between groups. The overlap is considerable. The similarities between males and females are too frequently ignored; the null hypothesis cannot be proved, and most journals publish only significant results.

Other biases are found in the material presented in introductory texts. Many texts report the same research (Do they copy from each other?), which comes from traditional sources such as APA journals. Because feminist research is not always acceptable to traditional reviewers (Denmark, 1977a), it gets published in more specialized outlets such as *Psychology of Women Quarterly (PWQ)* or *Sex Roles*. These sources are rarely cited by authors of introductory texts.

Questions have been raised about whether or not there is, or should be, feminist research methodology. There are diverse opinions about this, but I agree with Barbara Wallston (Note 3) that no one method is inherently feminist. Indeed, a variety of methods is necessary to fully explore the psychology of women. Our theories and the questions we researchers ask, as well as the interpretation of our data, can be feminist. However, the methods we use should be appropriate to our questions. Of course, we should be open to a variety of methods and not predetermine what is "scientific" and reject out-of-hand techniques that seem different or novel and therefore are automatically judged as less rigorous.

For those interested in methodological issues, I recommend a special section on feminist research in the *Psychology of Women Quarterly (PWQ)* edited by Virginia O'Leary (1981) with articles by Barbara Wallston, Robert Brannon, Kathleen Grady, Mary Parlee, and Rhoda Unger. Recent issues of the *Association for Women in Psychology (AWP) Newsletter* also contain a forum of readers' views on feminist research methodology (Leverone, 1981; Rheinhart, 1982; Sherif, 1982).

Moral Development From a Feminist Perspective

All texts and introductory courses include sections on moral development. But none of these sections present research on moral development beyond that of Kohlberg.

Since the 1960s, Lawrence Kohlberg has presented a theory of moral development that states that children progress through distinct stages of moral judgment that reflect developmental changes in the child's cognitive conceptions of morality (1976). These six stages occur in an invariant sequence whereby each stage develops out of and is more complex than the earlier ones. In Kohlberg's view, these stages are universal and characterize the development of moral thinking in people all over the world.

Although Kohlberg's variations on the Piagetian theme have made an important contribution to our understanding of the development of moral thought, recent criticisms have called some of his basic assumptions into question. One line of opposition has originated from Carol Gilligan (1977, 1979). She questions the assumptions of a hierarchy of moral dispositions in which highly educated white males have a disproportionate likelihood of coming out on top of the morality scale. In effect, this theory places Western men in a position of moral superiority so women naturally, as "the other," appear morally and otherwise inferior.

In fact, investigations into Kohlberg's work have shown that his theory of moral development was based exclusively on research with male subjects. When females were eventually tested, they rarely scored higher than three on a scale of six moral stages. Many females seemed to be stuck at the stage that would indicate that their sense of morality was related more to people than to abstract universal principles. Morality for women seemed to mean being responsible to oneself and to others, as opposed to doing one's duty or fulfilling one's obligations. Carol Gilligan investigated this male-oriented theory of moral development and concluded that there were two different, but equal, paths to morality—and women and men were clearly on different paths.

In order to find out how people would react to a naturally occurring moral situation, rather than to a far-fetched and hypothetical Kohlberg type where men were dominant characters, Gilligan and her associates interviewed women prior to their making a decision about having an abortion and then again a year later. They asked women to describe what conflicts were moral problems for them. They also asked men their views of this conflict. In general, men resolved the dilemma with a broad, impersonal ruling: Either abortion is murder and therefore is wrong, or the fetus does not acquire rights until birth and therefore abortion is a woman's right. Men slotted the conflict into a category and then applied a rule that would be true for all conflicts within that category. Women, on the other hand, took into account the specifics of the situation (i.e., the kind of relationship, if any, she had with the father, her finances, her health, etc.) and then made a decision. Women focused not so much on the right thing to do, but on the responsible thing to do. The women's responses clearly clashed with stage six on Kohlberg's scale, which is supposedly based on universal ethical principles. Men met stage six criteria by wanting to be noninterfering and independent. Women, on the other hand, related to morality through caring. Who, then, is more "moral?"

The answer lies in interpretation. Since many of the moral concerns women voiced fell through the sieve of male-based theories, they appear from this perspective to lie outside the moral domain. Gilligan argues that moral judgment depends on the way in which a moral problem is framed, and her evidence suggested that men and women frame them differently. The real problem emerges when the ways in which women express and evaluate morality are interpreted by psychologists as morally weak.

Gilligan's theory of morality gives a positive view of characteristics that have been continually disparaged. This theory emphasizes the value of people's attachments to others—human relationships are at the heart of the theory. For so long, all of these people concerns involving caring, relationships, work, respect for other people's feelings, and so forth were devalued because they were thought to be separate from the attributes of logic and reason, which were typically associated with men.

Gilligan believes that these two paths to morality are different but equal, and that there is nothing inherently better or worse in one than in the other. But they are different and the difference must be recognized.

Biological Foundations of Behavior and Sex Differences

Looking for biological foundations of behavior has proved to be one of the most exciting areas in psychology today. During the last decade, social scientists have accumulated an impressive amount of evidence that suggests that heredity and body chemistry play a large role in the determination of behavior. One would be hard pressed, for example, to find an explanation of manic depression or schizophrenia in which biological factors did not play a major role. I have recently read some popular, scholarly, and textbook accounts of some of these new research and theoretical developments in which authors have implied that feminists are against this type of research because it suggests that socialization has little or nothing to do with gender differences in behavior. Feminists, who favor a social explanation over a purely biological one, come off like sore losers or poor sports.

I discourage this thinking and refute it whenever it appears. First, feminists encourage research conducted in a nonsexist manner. Too often findings that indicate biological origins of gender differences also imply that social interventions are futile. This is simply not the case. Second, the nature/nurture controversy has been alive and well for thousands of years, and evidence continues to indicate that both influences, separately and together, have an impact on behavior. To promote one side over the other is, on a purely intellectual level, wrong. Biology does not cause behavior. Rather, biology and behavior both represent different levels of the same process. Influences on either level may affect the other. Textbooks and class discussions should make this point.

I will now examine several topics with underlying assumptions that are relevant to the psychology of women and to feminists and to a discussion of the biological foundations of behavior: sociobiology, hormonal influences on behavior, brain lateralization, and mathematical ability.

Sociobiology

Discussion of sociobiology has crept into textbooks during the last several years. If the topic does appear, students should be encouraged to examine the underlying assumptions. Because many of the assumptions can be related to psychoanalytic theory, it may be useful to consider both topics at the same time.

Sociobiology contends that complex social behavior such as aggression and passivity, success and failure, sympathy and callousness, stem from a genetic base. Edward O. Wilson (1975), the leading advocate of this approach, proposes that mechanisms of heredity underlie all social behavior and, furthermore, that this behavior attempts to ensure that only genes favoring survival are passed on. Social behavior prevails because of uncontrollable and unchangeable heredity factors.

Sociobiologists believe that gender differences in social and sexual behavior also have this evolutionary basis. By definition, social and sexual behavior are immune to situational and environmental influences. This analysis undermines the feminist position that much of this behavior is the product of social conditioning and is maintained by a subtle series of rewards and punishments (Taylor & Kabatznick, Note 4). Sociobiology asserts that this behavior reflects the natural order of things and thus implies that steps to modify it are useless. Women display weak social characteristics and men strong ones because of some fixed, predetermined genetic scheme. Feminists look ridiculous in their efforts to change views of biology and genetics, and, moreover, they appear demonic for wanting to change a course that favors the continuation and propagation of individuals and the human race.

Sociobiology, like psychoanalysis, may seem compelling because it has the capacity to explain any behavior. In reality, the sociobiological approach explains nothing. It simply labels phenomena that already exist. Scientific explanation demands that theorists provide a means of disproving one's hypothesis. How then can sociobiology explain the wide variety of female and male behavior that occurs cross-culturally? The entire analysis is post hoc and has no predictive capacity. Any gender-role norm can be justified because it exists. When gender-role norm changes occur, sociobiologists can then say these changes are due to some unforeseen gene that favors survival.

Sociobiology supports the "biology is destiny" mentality. Instead of accounting for women's subordinate position in society with androcentric concepts like penis envy and inadequate superego, sociobiologists simply use the language of biology. This gives the appearance that sociobiological theory is ultrascientific when in fact there is no empirical basis for such an approach. The language sounds good and has scientific prestige. Students should be aware of how language can influence people's perceptions.

Sociobiology, like psychoanalysis, supports the status quo instead of questioning it. Feminists believe that sociobiologists attempt to justify prevailing gender-role norms that discriminate against women.

Hormonal Influences on Behavior

The search for biological differences that affect behavior in females and males has gone on for years. Most recent attempts to locate variations have focused on the hypothalamus and more recently on the shape and surface of the corpus callosum. Much of the regulation of female and male sexual arousal and behavior takes place in the hypothalamus, although the exact areas vary across species. Hypothalamic areas, however, seem to be structured differently for each sex (Leshner, 1978). Recent studies have shown that the structural differences in the brains of females and males are caused by different hormone exposure in early development. However, does evidence such as this necessarily indicate that biology is responsible for all of the variations found between females and males?

Certainly not. Virtually all of these studies were conducted on animals and say little more about behavior than that there are brain controls for fertility cycles in females and for sexual interest in both sexes. Some would suggest that this could account for such diverse human behavior as occupational choice and athletic interest, but currently there is no foundation for such beliefs. Social factors exert powerful influences on behavior and cannot be ignored or denied. When discussing this material, I usually ask students to indicate what social rules society sets for male and female sexual behavior that could account for other variations in female and male behavior.

This is not to suggest that feminists dismiss hormonal and biological differences. What is at issue here is the quality of interpretation. What I object to are discussions that support biological determinants of behavior and cite evidence to argue that females and males behave differently primarily, if not exclusively, because of these determinants. These authors acknowledge in a few fleeting sentences that there are criticisms and alternative approaches to this thinking, but do not elaborate on these or include evidence that would contradict the approach or theory in question.

As I noted before, much of the evidence that supports biological factors as the fundamental basis for differences in female and male behavior is based on animal studies. There are rare cases, however, in which certain things that are done to animals in experimental situations do occur in humans as a result of glandular defects or the use of certain drugs. By examining some of these cases, we can take a closer look at how social factors influence these so-called biological determinants. For example, sometimes a female is exposed to an excess of androgens before birth and may even have masculinized genitals at the time of birth, which are usually corrected surgically. This condition, prenatal androgenization, is supposed to have an effect on the woman's behavioral disposition. In 1973, Anke Ehrhardt and Susan

Baker studied 17 girls with this condition and compared them with their sisters. The purpose of the study, which is frequently cited in introductory textbooks, was to find out how the sisters differed behaviorally. Any difference could then be interpreted as being caused by the girls' excess exposure to male hormones. The researchers concluded that these girls tended to act in more tomboyish ways than their sisters. They liked outdoor sports "more" and were "somewhat more likely to start fights."

In a few of the books I examined, the conclusion to this study stated that although these data are not conclusive, they suggest that the male hormones may have predisposed these girls to behave more aggressively. And that was that. How then can tomboyish girls who do not have prenatal androgenization be explained? Why is this critical question ignored? Why are social factors, such as parental attitudes toward daughters with this condition, not discussed as a possible source of these supposedly marked behavioral differences? When omissions like these occur, authors create a bias that is undeserved. My informal analysis of introductory textbooks shows that this bias more often favors males than females.

Brain Lateralization

Recent research on brain lateralization has indicated that males have more right-hemispheric dominance than females. In behavioral terms, this means that males are supposed to excel in mechanics and mathematical skills. Females, on the other hand, are supposed to outperform males on tasks relating to language and integrative skills because of their left-hemispheric dominance. Moreover, there is evidence indicating that females are less lateralized than males because the female brain may have had less time to develop hemispheric differentiation during puberty. This could indicate that females are predisposed to a broad range of abilities because they have a larger area of the brain from which to draw dominant skills. If this is not technically correct it at least seems like a reasonable alternate interpretation. Why then do many reviewers and authors conclude simply that females are consistently less able than males?

Some writers have even gone so far as to say that with less interference from the left or "female" side of the brain, men could then use their right hemisphere more precisely. Why not state that with less interference from the right or "male" side of the brain, women could use their left hemisphere more precisely? I find that posing these types of questions is particularly instructive and enlightening.

Mathematical Ability

An issue of particular interest to students is the great mathematical ability debate that has been raging among psychologists during the last two years. Camilla Benbow and Julian Stanley published a study (1980) affirming what many people apparently want to believe: Sex differences in mathematics are partly biological in origin and so, by implication, are beyond educational influence. The authors concluded this after comparing the 1972 and 1979 Scholastic Aptitude Test (SAT) math scores of 10,000 seventh and eighth grade students. These equal numbers of females and males had received, according to the authors, "essentially" the same training and had demonstrated talent in math. After examining the scores, the researchers found that males scored higher than females. What caught everybody's interest and generated such controversy was the authors' interpretation:

> We favor the hypothesis that sex differences in achievement and attitude toward mathematics result from superior male ability, which may in turn be related to greater male ability in spatial tasks. This male superiority is probably an expression of a combination of both endogenous and exogenous variables (p. 1264).

Although the Benbow and Stanley study did not include a study of biological factors, many readers embraced their findings and interpretations as definitive, specifically that mathematical ability is innate and beyond social influences. But what about reports that indicate that sex-related differences could also be explained by environmental factors?

A number of researchers found that in some math achievement studies, the number of courses taken by boys and girls had indeed not been held constant, contrary to Benbow and Stanley's claim of essentially equal training. In fact, one of my doctoral students at the City University of New York, Jody Altenhof (Note 5), examined the 1978 and 1979 SAT scores of females and males for sex differences in all ability levels. Before the number of years of math courses was held constant, her preliminary analysis indicated that males did perform better in math, especially in geometry. Based on her sample, when the years of math courses were held constant, no overall significant sex differences were found between females and males. These findings about geometry suggest that there may not be a math difference per se between females and males, but a difference in visual-spatial abilities.

Benbow and Stanley not only handled their data inadequately, they also did not take into account other influential environmental factors that could have accounted for their findings. Things such as gender-preferential parental attitudes toward math, math-related play for boys, and out-of-school experience in problem solving undoubtedly play some role in how children perform in gender-related tasks (Denmark, Note 6). Unless Benbow and Stanley could show that their subjects had identical exposure to, attitudes toward, and experiences with math, their conclusion that there is a genetic basis to this ability appears unreasonable. If their findings were conclusive, how could Sheila Tobias (1982) report that a dramatic shift in the number of female PhDs in math has occurred over the last ten years? In 1970, only 6% went to women and by 1980 the number of mathematical PhDs awarded to women had risen to 14%. Since we do know that numerous social factors influence women's participation in certain tasks, it seems reasonable to focus on these in order to minimize female and male mathematical discrepancies. Establishing math anxiety clinics and encouraging females to take more math courses are two ways of dealing with this.

Personality and Mental Health Issues

Discussions of personality theory are rarely criticized from a feminist perspective. Students may read that concepts like penis envy and the Oedipal complex are too broad and intangible for research purposes, but they rarely read that the terms also denigrate females by implying that the male is the norm. Nor do students learn that the principle of unconscious motivation underlies many popular and judicial attitudes towards rape survivors (Sherman, 1980), battered women (Leidig, 1981), and even incest victims (Herman & Hirschman, 1977).

The psychoanalytic perspective encourages negative reactions toward female sexuality and the female sex role by insisting that women are doomed to act out a set of socially undesirable personality traits because of penis envy (Kabatznick, Note 7). Theories such as those proposed by Clara Thompson (1964), Karen Horney (1939), and Benjamin Wolman (1975) account for this analysis by advocating that men need to make women look jealous and envious because of their own inability to deal with womb and breast envy. I believe that these theories are ignored because of an ambivalence toward explanations of behavior in which men are cast in inferior and demeaning positions.

Erik Erikson's work on inner and outer space (1964) is always covered under personality theories in introductory textbooks. Students learn that the shape of the genitals in each sex is somehow translated into a profound difference in the sexes' sense of space—an assumption that nicely supports the Freudian biology-is-destiny theme. It is rarely pointed out that the basis for Erikson's theory was one poorly controlled study (which has never been rigorously replicated) in which 140 boys and girls between 11 and 13 years of age built imaginary scenes out of a selection of toys. Although Erikson did not account for prior experience with blocks, his interpretation that boys built towers and girls built enclosures because of their sex organs has become part of the collective wisdom of psychology.

Similarly, many other traditional personality theorists and personality-test developers have declared that biologically women and men must embody all of the attendant stereotypic feminine or masculine traits in order to be labeled healthy and well-adjusted. Masculinity and femininity were seen as polar opposites mutually exclusive of each other. Women and men who acted out of role were labeled sick because these psychologists focused on whether behavior was typically masculine or feminine rather than on whether or not it was appropriate to the situation.

More recent work by Sandra Bem (1974) and Janet Spence and Robert Helmreich (1978) has indicated that people are not compelled to behave entirely as either males or females but can behave as both. This personality characteristic, known as psychological androgyny, is defined as the possession of high degrees of both masculine and feminine personality characteristics. Therefore, androgynous individuals should be able to demonstrate either instrumental or expressive behavior as the situation or context demands and in this sense show behavioral flexibility. In fact, some research studies have shown that androgynous individuals of both sexes have higher levels of social competence and self-esteem than individuals who are sex-typed or undifferentiated (Gilbert, 1980). On the other hand, androgyny should not be considered a mental health ideal (Gilbert, 1980). Certainly, sex-typed individuals can be healthy and adjusted as long as sex-typed behavior does not interfere with their levels of functioning. Furthermore, people could score as very androgynous and still be stereotypic in their judgments about others.

Yet evidence shows that women and men are expected to adhere to traditional gender-role norms in the psychotherapeutic situation. Women and men who act out of role are labeled sicker than when they exhibit behavior that conforms to rigid gender-role stereotypes. Kathleen Kelly and Sandra Kiersky, two doctoral students at the City University of New York, investigated clinicians' judgments of pathology as a function of sex and symptomology (Note 8). Fifty practicing psychotherapists participated in the study. Videotapes were produced using female and male actors posing as patients exhibiting aggressive or passive behavior. It was hypothesized that clinicians would judge the aggressive female as more severely disturbed than the aggressive male and the depressed female as less disturbed than the depressed male. The results showed that in-role patient behavior was judged less severely on a number of measures than was out-of-role behavior, but this effect was found primarily among male clinicians. Male clinicians were more likely than were female clinicians to judge the depressed male, compared to the depressed female, as psychotic. Male clinicians were also more likely to perceive both female and male out-of-role patients as more severely ill than in-role patients. Finally, they were more likely to recommend medication for the depressed male than for the depressed female.

This evidence demonstrates that male and female patients are often treated, especially by male clinicians, according to how closely they adhere to or deviate from conservative gender-role norms. Other studies indicate that women are more likely to be diagnosed as depressed (Weissman & Klerman, 1981), are more likely to receive tranquilizing medication, and are more likely to be hospitalized (Cooperstock, 1971) than are males. Does this mean that women are sicker than men? Maybe they are, but several factors should be considered when discussing the outcome of such studies.

Perhaps there are greater stresses intrinsic to the female role than are recognized. Or maybe women are more willing to disclose problems than are men and are therefore more willing to seek and be referred for treatment. On the other hand, these findings may reflect prevailing beliefs that women are passive, dependent, and emotional.

Suicide is another mental health issue that often inspires sexist interpretation. My work with Ronna Kabatznick (Denmark & Kabatznick, 1981) showed that some researchers interpret the fact that women attempt suicide more often than men but are less likely to succeed as evidence that these women were not really serious about dying. Factors such as the limited access women have to violent weapons and their relative lack of experience (compared to men's) in acting in physically aggressive ways are virtually ignored.

Feminist therapy is a method of treatment that takes into account the gender-role norms that discriminate against women. But it is rarely mentioned in chapters on psychotherapy, despite the fact that females constitute the majority of psychotherapy consumers today. Yet these chapters always contain information on Freud and psychoanalysis. Less certain but predictable are sections on client-centered therapy and behavior modification techniques. More recently, I have seen information included that runs the gamut from European imagery methods (treating intrapsychic conflicts through reliance on imagery associations), to flooding or implosion, to methods that require patients to imagine or confront their most feared scenes or actions. But where is feminist therapy?

Now that it is evident that psychotherapy is not the value-free system it was once thought to be and that numerous methods may encourage women to adhere to the very behavior causing their personal problems (Denmark & Block, 1980), students should be aware that there are alternatives to traditional treatments. Feminist therapy and nonsexist therapy allow "clients to determine their own destinies without the constriction of culturally prescribed sex-role stereotypes based upon assumed biological differences. Both approaches attempt to facilitate equality (in personal power) between females and males" (Rawlings & Carter, 1977, p. 50). Yet, despite the overlap, psychologists distinguish between the two methods.

The major distinction between feminist and nonsexist therapy is that feminist therapy incorporates the values and philosophy of feminism—that females and males should have equal opportunities for gaining personal, political, and economic power. Feminist therapy also insists that interactions between persons should be egalitarian and not based on some subjective norm. In fact, nonsexist therapists may be feminist in their beliefs, but if these are not transmitted in the therapy, then feminist therapy is not being practiced. For example, many standard norms of treatment—such as silence and passivity—are not held in high esteem by feminist therapists.

Feminist therapy also maintains that the therapeutic relationship should not involve inequities in power. Women have been trained to be helpless and dependent and the last thing they need is to have their dependence encouraged, exploited, or prolonged by a therapist.

Furthermore, feminist therapy focuses on the social factors that instigate pathology. Unlike psychoanalysis, feminist therapy attributes the primary source of people's problems to social factors that are external to the individual. This focus on environmental stress does not deny the importance of individual responsibility. On the contrary, feminist therapy encourages women to become economically and psychologically independent so that they can, in turn, effect social and political changes that will alleviate women's oppressed state.

The woman who is undergoing feminist therapy typically gains insight into the external forces that have shaped her behavior and have pushed her into using powerless, stereotypically feminine behavior. Feminist therapy is concerned with women's lack of power and the problems women face simply by being women.

The goals of feminist therapy include identifying obstacles to growth and helping women grow and have fulfilling lives. Sometimes this may mean that women will recognize that drastic life-style and social change are necessary. The feminist therapist would oppose all forces that pressure the client to accept and adjust to the status quo. Specific techniques used by the feminist therapist include consciousness raising and assertiveness training.

I have found two sources particularly useful for students. The first, *Women and Psychotherapy: A Consumer Handbook,* was prepared by the Task Force on Consumer Issues in Psychotherapy of the Association for Women in Psychology and the Division of the Psychology of Women of the APA (Liss-Levinson et al., 1982). This pamphlet summarizes some of the major issues surrounding women and therapy and provides students with information about various forms of therapy. The second source is the Report of the Task Force on Sex Bias and Sex-Role Stereotyping in Psychotherapeutic Practice, published in the December 1975 issue of the *American Psychologist* (Brodsky & Holroyd). Class discussions of the many points made in this article have proven valuable.

Obviously, every mental issue relevant to women cannot be covered here. Other important issues that should be included are eating disorders, phobic disorders (especially agoraphobia), and the psychological impact of mastectomy.

I would also like to point out that always covering certain topics in mental health units can create unfounded biases. The psychological effects of abortion, divorce, and the empty nest period (erroneously labeled the empty nest "syndrome") are topics often covered in these units, which suggests that these experiences go hand in hand with psychological difficulties. In fact, there are a host of studies indicating that women do not undergo the strains that many have suggested. Similarly, many discussions on lesbian women imply that their psychological problems are the result of their sexual orientation. How absurd it would be to suggest that a heterosexual's personal problems stemmed from sexual preferences.

Women and Social Behavior

As a social psychologist, I find this subject the most difficult to cover—not for lack of material, but because my familiarity with it makes it difficult to select what should be included in this brief discussion.

As noted earlier, I will not focus on prejudice and stereotypes, except to note that in teaching the introductory course, the instructor should point out the double bind of minority women. Black and hispanic women, for example, are subject to the constraints of both racism and sexism; lesbian women are subject to the constraints of both sexism and homophobia. If an instructor talks about mass media, then gender-role stereotyping should be a major component of this discussion. Rape, sexual harassment, and violence against women should certainly be considered in any discussion of aggression and power.

If achievement motivation and behavior are considered, it is important that instructors point out that barriers to achievement may be internal—"a motive to avoid success"—but that many social factors also operate as barriers to women's success. Even when women succeed, reasons attributed to their success are different than those attributed to men. Women are more likely to be judged as lucky or to have worked hard; men are considered more skillful (Deaux &

Emswiller, 1974). For those who discuss Matina Horner's "fear of success" (1972), it should be pointed out that many men, as well as women, have a motive to avoid success. Recent studies indicate that women and men score similarly on Horner's "Mary" or "John" cue (Tresemer, 1976, 1977). The percentage of women who are judged to be motivated by this fear has dropped considerably, whereas the percentage of men has shown a considerable increase. It should also be noted that Horner's single projective cue has been the target of methodological criticism (e.g., Denmark, Tangri, & McCandless, 1978). Horner's later work with several colleagues (Note 9) includes three verbal cues:

1. Carol is walking along the beach late in the day . . .
2. Joan is looking into her microscope . . .
3. After much effort, Anne has finally gotten what she wanted . . .

A topic that I feel should be included whenever covering social psychology is the relationship between power, gender, and status— including women and leadership. Social power refers to the access to and use of institutional and other human resources for the effective initiation and control of social interaction. Until recently, women's roles in social power have usually been ignored. Only men were discussed under this heading. The lack of a gender variable in studies of power, status, and leadership points to the gaps in existing research and theoretical models. In a paper given at the 1982 Psychological Association, Rhoda Unger (Note 10) discussed some of the factors that led to this remarkable oversight in studies of power and status: (a) the culturally based assumption that power has not been an important motivator and the contradictory assumption that it should be, (b) the tendency for psychologists not to seek or find differences in power and status because of the laboratory setting in which these variables were studied, (c) the tendency of American psychologists to look for intrapsychic rather than social explanations for power and status, and (d) the tendency for Americans to be unaware of the extent to which power and status influence their own behavior.

Unger believes that the social-psychological study of sex differences has led to renewed interest in status and power, and she attributes this development to two facts. (a) Sex and status are often confounded, a point also made by the late Carolyn Wood Sherif (Note 11). In other words, many behaviors ascribed to sex differences may actually be caused or influenced by status or power differences. (b) Psychologists are using more field experiments and unobtrusive measures, which permit examinations of ongoing relationships. Thus, psychologists now have access to behavior measures other than the paper and pencil measures of the laboratory.

Certainly Nancy Henley's work (1977) on the politics of touch and interpersonal space has led us to a greater understanding of how power and status are nonverbally generated and maintained. I have found that students respond very positively to this material because they can observe themselves and others engaging in the behaviors known to communicate status. For example, it has been noted that persons occupying low-status positions smile, nod, gaze downward, and maintain a more rigid posture than do high-status individuals. Low-status individuals are also more likely to be the recipients of non-reciprocal touching. Similarly, low-status people are much more likely to be called by their first names than are high-status people. All of these tendencies have been found by Henley to be more common among women than among men.

Wendy McKenna and I (Denmark, 1977b; Note 12) conducted a study to test whether women's perceived status varies as a function of the nonverbal behavior they exhibit. We wanted to learn what happens if a woman engages in the high-status behavior typically associated with men. Is she perceived as more competent and as possessing greater authority? Or does her gender dominate her behavior? In condensed form, the findings revealed that male and female respondents arrived at evaluations on the basis of the confederate's nonverbal behavior rather than on the basis of sex. In other words, when women displayed high-status nonverbal behavior, respondents evaluated the women as having higher status; when women displayed low-status nonverbal behavior, they were considered to have low status. The implication of this study is that, when women project themselves as competent through nonverbal techniques, they are more likely to be perceived accordingly.

Another study in which McKenna and I collaborated (Note 13) used the small world technique devised by Stanley Milgram to investigate the social communication networks within the field of psychology (see Korte & Milgram, 1970; Milgram, 1967; Travers & Milgram, 1969). We wanted to investigate systematically whether the informal chains that exist within most professions exclude women in the field of psychology.

In our adaptation of the small world technique we sent information about a target person to 800 individuals, both psychologists and nonpsychologists. The targets were all male and female psychologists who were categorized as high or low status on the basis of their professional affiliations and positions. Each of the starters, as we called the 800 individuals, was required to forward a booklet they had been sent to another person they knew on a first-name basis and whom they believed might be personally acquainted with the target. This process continued, when the senders complied, until the booklet finally reached the target person.

A preliminary analysis of this data has suggested some interesting things about gender and status. More male than female target chains were completed regardless of target status (the average chain was 3.48

links, which was actually two links shorter than Milgram's reported chain lengths). However, completed chain lengths were similar for both male and female targets, although they were shorter for high-status targets than for low-status targets. Thus status, not gender, makes a difference in chain length.

Another finding indicated that female psychologists were more successful than their nonpsychologist counterparts in reaching the target person. Our findings also indicated that those who had direct access to high-status men and women were most often male. Thus, people turn to men to reach high-status males.

This study has broad implications. It appears that when people want to reach high-status others, they think of men. The gender and status differences we found do not necessarily come from the deliberate exclusion of women. They come from more subtle factors, such as advisers being more likely to contact male students than female students. These results show that women are more isolated than men, although the characteristic of this isolation varies with the status of the woman. It is a small world—smaller for some than for others.

Conclusion

I hope that I have helped clarify the relationship of the psychology of women to the study of psychology. I have specifically pointed out some topics that should be considered in an introductory psychology course. For a more in-depth coverage of the psychology of women, refer to the Suggested Reading list on page 61, which includes some basic texts and papers. I also recommend an instrument for assessing information about sex differences in the introductory psychology courses, which was designed by Nancy Russo and Natalie Malavich (1982). A collection of awareness and assertiveness training exercises has also been appended to this essay. These exercises, grouped by topic, can be used by instructors to illustrate points relevant to the psychology of women. By participating in such exercises students should become more aware of issues in the psychology of women important for introductory psychology.

As the psychology of women continues to develop, it will have more and more impact on introductory psychology—the texts, the instructors, and the students. I hope psychology instructors will be in the forefront and facilitate this impact, so that students will realize that the psychology of women is a respectable, scholarly, and established field within the discipline of psychology.

Suggested Reading

Articles

Denmark, F. L. The psychology of women: An overview of an emerging field. *Personality and Social Psychology Bulletin,* 1977, *3,* 356–367.

Mednick, M. T. S. Psychology of women: Research issues and trends. *Annals of the New York Academy of Science,* 1978, *3098,* 77–92.

Parlee, M. B. Review essay: Psychology. *Signs,* 1975, *1,* 119–138.

Unger, R. K. Toward a redefinition of sex and gender. *American Psychologist,* 1979, *34* (11), 1085–1094.

Vaughter, R. M. Review essay: Psychology. *Signs,* 1976, 2, 120–146.

Handbooks and Collections

Cox, S. (Ed.). *Female psychology: The emerging self* (2nd. ed.). New York: St. Martin's Press, 1981.

Denmark, F. L. (Ed.). *Women: A PDI research reference work (Vol. 1).* New York: Psychological Dimensions, 1976.

Kaplan, A. G., & Bran, J. P. (Eds.) *Beyond sex-role stereotypes: Readings toward a psychology of adrogyny.* Boston: Little, Brown, 1976.

Sherman, J. A., & Denmark, F. L. (Eds.). *The psychology of women: Future directions in research.* New York: Psychological Dimensions, 1978.

Unger, R. K., & Denmark, F. L. (Eds.). *Women: Dependent or independent variable?* New York: Psychological Dimensions, 1975.

Textbooks

Basow, S. A. *Sex-role stereotypes: Traditions and alternatives.* Monterey, CA: Brooks/Cole, 1980.

Deaux, K. *The behavior of women and men.* Monterey, CA: Brooks/Cole, 1976.

Donelson, F. E., & Gullahorn, J. E. *Women: A psychological perspective.* New York: Wiley, 1977.

Frieze, I. H., Parsons, J. E., Johnson, P. B., Ruble, D. N., & Zellman, G. L. *Women sex roles: Pressure points in the lives of women.* New York: Norton, 1978.

Hyde, J. S., & Rosenberg, B. G. *Half the human experience* (2nd ed.). Lexington, MA: Heath, 1980.

O'Leary, V. E. *Toward understanding women.* Monterey, CA: Brooks/Cole.

Rohrbaugh, J. B. *Women: Psychology's puzzle.* New York: Basic Books, 1980.

Tavris, C. A., & Offir, C. W. *The longest war: Sex differences in perspective.* New York: Harcourt Brace Jovanovich, 1977.

Unger, R. K. *Female and male: Psychological perspective.* New York: Harper & Row, 1979.

Williams, J. H. *The psychology of women* (2nd ed.). New York: Norton, 1982.

Awareness Exercises

Women in Mid-Life

1. What makes a woman seem old? What makes a woman seem young?

2. What are appropriate activities for a middle-aged or older woman?

3. Why is the "empty nest" period welcomed by some women?

4. How do the adjustments faced by older women affect their mental health?

Stereotypes

1. What functions do sex-role stereotypes serve?

2. How does language support sex-role stereotypes?

Sex-Role Development

1. Is the English language sexist? How does sexist language affect a child and "his" development?

2. Does school play a part in the acquisition of sex stereotypes in children? How? Do female children feel they are treated differently by their teachers than do boys?

3. Is a child's behavior derived from imitation, reinforcement, and observational learning as it is postulated by social learning theorists?

Achievement

1. Do you consider yourself an achievement-oriented person? What aspects of your childhood do you feel helped facilitate this orientation? If you do not consider yourself achievement oriented, what aspects of your childhood may have prevented this?

2. What characterizes a person as an achiever or a success? Are there differences in achievement needs for males and females?

3. According to Horner, bright, achieving women often experience a "fear of success." Have you ever experienced a fear of success or a conflict in your desire to pursue a career? At what age would fear of success be most prevalent?

4. Attribution researchers have found sex differences in attributions for failure. Do you think the women's movement has helped women to attribute failure unstably or externally?

Women and Work

1. Does affirmative action cause more problems than it solves?

2. What are the advantages and disadvantages of being the only woman in a corporate setting?

Continued

3. A woman in the corporate arena is conspicuous. How should a woman act in such a situation? Should she attempt to blend in, stay in the background, or should she take advantage of her novelty? Whatever tactic you choose will probably have different implications for what might be considered feminist goals, as opposed to personal goals. Which sets of goals should be given priority? What are some of the implications of choosing one set of goals over the other?

4. Do interpersonal relationships vary between sexes?

5. What advantages might women perceive to gain by remaining in subservient positions in either the work or the marriage situation?

Marriage

1. Tasks in marriage are still generally divided along stereotypical lines. Men are becoming responsible for some traditionally feminine tasks, whereas women are not performing masculine tasks. Why? Will this change?

2. How much power do women have in the family? Is there a relationship between the relative power of men and women in the family during marriage and motherhood and the increasing divorce rate?

Motherhood

1. Is there a practical and effective approach that can be used to convince a traditionally raised man that fathering should and could be synonymous with mothering? Can a traditionally raised woman function as an equal partner in the responsibility and chores associated with raising a family without feeling guilty?

2. Do you think it is possible for a mother to return to or continue being the person she was before pregnancy?

3. Describe three goals (a) your mother had for you, (b) your father had for you, and (c) you have for your children. Do you have different goals for male and female children?

Learned Helplessness Theory

1. Might the learned helplessness theory suggest some solutions to the problem of why women in our society have accepted roles detrimental to their well-being?

Androgyny

1. Think of adjectives that are neither masculine nor feminine and that could describe the androgynous individual.

2. What are the implications to the androgynous individual for child-rearing practices?

Continued

3. There are many assumptions about the positive values associated with androgyny. What might some negative aspects of such a personality description be?

4. Look at the Bem Sex-Role Inventory and see if you can identify the sex-stereotyped adjectives and rate their social desirability. How do you rate yourself?

Leadership

1. What makes a woman become a leader? Discuss some of the different views about women as leaders.

2. Examine a number of factors such as talkativeness, leadership ability, intelligence, confidence, warmth, sensitivity, and so forth. How do these characteristics relate to leadership?

3. How should leaders be selected?

Awareness Exercises

Sex-Role Stereotypes

1. Go to the library, choose three books at random from the children's section, and look for sex-role stereotyping. Look at the illustrations. Who are the subjects and what are they doing?

2. Interview five males and five females and ask them to give traits describing themselves. Discuss the differences between the two lists.

3. Choose three different time periods of TV viewing time. Note whether the nature or content of the material, obvious or not, changes depending on the time of the day and the expected female audience the station expects.

4. Compare and contrast the images of men and women projected by *Cosmopolitan, Playboy,* and *Ms.*

Women and Psychotherapy

1. Interview five males and five females. Have them list the adjectives that seem most appropriate to either healthy men, healthy women, or healthy people.

2. Pick three clinical psychology textbooks and examine the way they treat women.

3. Interview a therapist of each sex. See what their conceptions of appropriate sex roles are.

Sex-Role Development

1. Ask five boys and five girls what they want to be when they grow up.

2. Interview several parents of school-age children. The parent of at least one boy and one girl must be included in the sample. Ask whether the children were sent to nursery school, at what age they walked to school alone, and at what age they could sleep away from home. (Be aware that this method is limited by people's memories.)

3. Observe mother-child interactions on a playground. How are autonomy and dependence reinforced? Is there a sex difference?

Sex Differences in Cognitive Functions

1. Compute grade point averages separately for all courses taken with male professors as compared with female professors.

2. Spend a half hour each with a mother of a female and a mother of a male infant. Keep track of the time each mother spends talking to each child.

Continued

3. On a scale of 1 to 10 rank how anxious you are before taking an exam. Note sex differences in admitted anxiety. (Does the admission of anxiety demonstrate anxiety?)

4. Visit classes for children with learning disabilities. What sorts of impairments are found and what are their sex ratios?

Menstruation and Pregnancy

1. Keep daily records of your moods for two months, noting any fluctuations. Females should note on which days they are menstruating.

2. Interview three women at their time of ovulation and menstruation. Are there any reported or observable differences in moods between these segments?

Female Achievement

1. Review the obituary columns of a newspaper every day for a specified period and note the number of females and the number of males listed and what their accomplishment or status was that warranted an obituary.

2. Interview five women who have been successful in one field: music, athletics, business, the arts. What are the factors in their personal histories that explain their high achievement motivation?

3. Compare the occupational goals parents desire for their male and female children. Are there any sex differences on the basis of religion, ethnic group, or socioeconomic status?

Female Sexual Behavior

1. Ask five males and five females about their sexual fantasies. Is there a sex difference in response?

2. Define the term "rape." Interview several police officers on the subject. Do they believe rape is possible?

Note. From *Woman: Dependent or Independent Variable*, R. K. Unger and F. L. Denmark (Eds.), New York: Psychological Dimensions, 1975. Copyright 1975 by Psychological Dimensions. Adapted by permission.

Assertiveness Training Exercises

These role-playing exercises can be used to help students understand the issues relevant to assertiveness training and androgynous behavior.

Each situation presents students with a specific dilemma. The purpose of the exercise is to get the student to behave in ways that 1) are appropriate to the situation and 2) build a powerbase that reflects the person's sense of integrity and self-esteem.

Before the role-playing begins, read the issue aloud and ask students to list which behaviors would be the least appropriate for the conflicted person to engage in and have the students explain why this is so. Then ask them if this inappropriate behavior fits a female or male sex-role stereotype.

After the role-playing has taken place, ask the students who participated to explain how they felt. Then ask the observers to explain how they interpreted the various strategies used in trying to resolve the dilemma. What implications do they have for women?

These exercises help students develop personal coping strategies in difficult, and oftentimes, no win situations.

1. Your (lover, boyfriend, husband) wants you to take fewer college credits than you do. Each semester you have an argument and you always end up taking half the number of credits you wanted. This time you are not going to give in. You are going to take the number of credits you want AND you are going to keep the relationship going. How are you going to handle the situation?

2. Every time you and your friends get together, you end up doing what they want. Sometimes this means getting home very late and spending more money than you have to spend. You don't want to seem like a stick-in-the-mud, and then again you don't want to be both exhausted and broke. You're on the phone with one of your friends right now, and you've just been asked to join a bunch of people later on. How do you handle this situation?

3. Your boss has expected you to work every Saturday and for two months you've been doing so. You're tired of it. You don't want to work every Saturday and for those Saturdays you do, you want some kind of compensation (e.g. overtime pay, or an extra day off). The boss is notoriously difficult to deal with, and you know it. Basically, you like the job and the money is good so you discount the option to quit. You are just about to knock on the door of the boss. What are you going to say?

4. Your children have just asked you if they can stay up and watch a late night television show and you've said a firm, "No." Minutes later you hear their father say, "Yes" to the very same request. The children end up watching the program. You don't want this to happen again, and you feel the problem is more with the father than it is with the children. You want to tell the father that you feel your authority is being undermined when he does this. How would you do so in order to make sure this kind of thing won't happen again.

Note. Adapted by permission of R. Kabatznick.

Reference Notes

1. Holbrook, J. E. *Women and sex roles: Review from introductory psychology textbooks.* Paper presented at the meeting of the American Psychological Association, Washington, DC, 1982.
2. Furumoto, L. *Women in American psychology: An attempt to reconstruct the experience of the first generation (1890–1920).* Paper presented at the meeting of the Eastern Psychological Association, Baltimore, April 1982.
3. Horner, M. S., Tresemer, D. W., Berens, A. E., & Watson, R. I. *Scoring manual for an empirically derived scoring system for the motive to avoid success.* Unpublished manuscript, Harvard, 1973.
4. Taylor, C. J., & Kabatznick, R. *Onlooker responses to female and male runners.* Paper presented at the meeting of the American Psychological Association, Montreal, September 1980.
5. Altenhof, J. *Item characteristic influences male/female performance on SAT-M.* Unpublished dissertation research, 1982.
6. Denmark, F. L. *Research context of studies for sex differences in mathematics.* Paper presented at the meeting of the American Association for the Advancement of Science, Washington, DC, January 1982.
7. Kabatznick, R. *Actual and perceived options: A social psychological approach to interpersonal abuse and masochism.* Paper presented at the meeting of the American Psychological Association, Montreal, September 1980.
8. Kelly, K., & Kiersky, S. *Psychotherapists and sexual stereotypes: A study of bias in diagnostic interviews employing videotape simulations.* Paper presented at the meeting of the New York State Psychological Association, Saratoga, May 1979.
9. Wallston, B. S. *Feminist research methodology from a psychological perspective.* Paper presented at the first International Disciplinary Congress on Women, Haifa, Israel, December 1981.
10. Unger, R. *Controlling out the obvious: Power, status and social psychology.* Paper presented at the annual meeting of the American Psychological Association, Washington, DC, August 1982.
11. Sherif, C. W. *The web of social power and gender categories.* Unpublished manuscript, 1982.
12. McKenna, W., & Denmark, F. L. *Gender and nonverbal behavior as cues to status and power.* Paper presented at the meeting of the New York Academy of Sciences, New York, 1978.
13. Denmark, F. L., & McKenna, W. *The small world revisited: Informal communications network in psychology.* Paper presented at the American Psychological Association, Los Angeles, August 1981.

References

Bem, S. The measurement of psychological androgyny. *Journal of Clinical and Consulting Psychology,* 1974, *42,* 155–162.

Benbow, C., & Stanley, J. Sex differences in mathematical ability: Fact or artifact? *Science,* 1980, *210,* 1262–1264.

Berry, J. W. Temme and Eskimo perceptual skills. *International Journal of Psychology,* 1966, *1,* 207–229.

Brannon, R. Current methodological issues in paper and pencil measuring instruments. *Psychology of Women Quarterly,* 1981, *5,* 618–627.

Brodsky, A., & Holroyd, J. Report of the task force on sex bias and sex-role stereotyping in psychotherapeutic practice. *American Psychologist,* 1975, *30,* 1169–1175.

Cooperstock, R. Sex differences in the use of mood-modifying drugs: An explanatory model. *Journal of Health and Social Behavior,* 1971, *12,* 238–244.

Cox, W. M., Huselid, J. L., Johnson, C. M., Kavanagh, T. A., Phillips, K. M., & Swenson, B. M. Why students take general psychology. JSAS *Catalog of Selected Documents in Psychology,* 1982, *12,* 1. (Ms. No. 2403)

Deaux, K., & Emswiller, T. Explanations of successful performance on sex-linked tasks: What is skill for the male is luck for the female. *Journal of Personality and Social Psychology,* 1974, *29,* 80–85.

Denmark, F. L. The psychology of women: An overview of an emerging field. *Personality and Social Psychology Bulletin,* 1977a, *3,* 356–367.

Denmark, F. L. Styles of leadership. *Psychology of Women Quarterly,* 1977b, *2,* 99–112.

Denmark, F. L. Psyche: From rocking the cradle to rocking the boat. *American Psychologist,* 1980, *12,* 1057–1065.

Denmark, F. L., & Block, J. The psychodynamics of women (Pts. 1 & 2). *Weekly Psychology Update,* 1980, *1* (7–8), 1–8, 1–8.

Denmark, F. L., & Kabatznick, R. Women and suicide. In F. F. Flach (Ed.), *Directions in Psychiatry.* New York: Hatherleigh, 1981.

Denmark, F. L., Tangri, S. S., & McCandless, S. Affiliation, achievement and power: A new look. In J. A. Sherman and F. L. Denmark (Eds.), *The Psychology of Women: Future Directions in Research.* New York: Psychological Dimensions, 1978.

Erhardt, A., & Baker, S. W. Fetal androgens, lunar central nervous system differentiation and behavior sex differences. In R. C. Friedman, R. M. Rutart, & R. L. Vande Wole (Eds.), *Sex differences in behavior.* New York: Wiley, 1973.

Erikson, E. H. Inner and outer space: Reflections on womanhood. *Daedalus,* 1964, *93,* 582–606.

Gilbert, L. A. Psychological androgyny and mental health. *Weekly Psychology Update,* 1980, *1* (9), 1–8.

Gilligan, C. In a different voice: Women's conceptions of self and of morality. *Harvard Educational Review,* 1977, *47,* 481–517.

Gilligan, C. Women's place in man's life cycle. *Harvard Educational Review,* 1979, *49,* 431–446.

Grady, K. Sex bias in research design. *Psychology of Women Quarterly,* 1981, *5,* 628–636.

Hall, G. S. *Coeducation.* American Academy of Medicine, 1906.

Henley, N. *Body politics.* Englewood Cliffs, NJ: Prentice-Hall, 1977.

Herman, J., & Hirschman, L. Incest between fathers and daughters. *The Sciences,* 1977, *17,* 4–7.

Horner, M. Towards an understanding of achievement related conflicts in women. *Journal of Social Issues,* 1972, *28,* 157–175.

Horney, K. *New warp in psychoanalysis.* New York: Norton, 1939.

Hyde, J., & Rosenberg, B. G. *Half the human experience* (2nd ed.). Lexington, MA: Heath, 1980.

Kohlberg, L. Moral stages and moralization. In T. Likona (Ed.), *Moral development and behavior.* New York: Holt, Rhinehart & Winston, 1976.

Korte, C., & Milgram, S. Acquaintance networks between racial groups: Applications of the small-world method. *Journal of Personality and Social Psychology,* 1970, *15,* 101–108.

Janda, L., & Klenke-Hamel, K. *Psychology: Its study and uses.* New York: St. Martin's Press, 1982.

Leidig, M. W. Violence against women: A feminist-psychological analysis. In S. Cox (Ed.), *Female psychology: The emerging self* (2nd ed.). New York: St. Martin's Press, 1981.

Leshner, A. I. *An introduction to behavioral endocrinology*. New York: Oxford University Press, 1978.

Leverone, J. Is there a feminist research methodology? *AWP Newsletter,* November–December 1981, p. 5.

Liss-Levinson, N., Clamar, A., Ehrenberg, M., Ehrenberg, O., Fidell, L., Maffeo, P., Redstone, J., Russo, N. F., Solomons, H., & Tennor, D. *Women and psychotherapy: A consumer handbook.* Washington, DC: Federation of Organizations for Professional Women, 1982.

Maccoby, E. E. The development of stimulus selection. In J. P. Hill (Ed.), *Minnesota Symposium of Child Development* (Vol. 3). 1969.

McKenna, W., & Kessler, S. Experimental design as a source of sex bias in social psychology. *Sex Roles,* 1977, *3,* 117–128.

Milgram, S. The small-world problem. *Psychology Today,* 1967, pp. 61–67.

O'Connell, A., & Russo, N. *Models of achievement: Reflections of eminent women in psychology.* New York: Columbia Press, 1983.

O'Leary, V. Feminist research: Problems and prospects. *Psychology of Women Quarterly,* 1981, *5,* 595–596.

Parlee, M. B. Appropriate control groups in feminist research. *Psychology of Women Quarterly,* 1981, *5,* 637–644.

Prescott, S. Why researchers don't study women: The responses of 62 researchers, *Sex Roles,* 1978, *4,* 899–905.

Rawlings, E., & Carter, D. K. *Psychotherapy for women.* Springfield, IL: Charles C Thomas, 1977.

Reinhart, N. Dilemmas in feminist methodology. *AWP Newsletter,* March–April 1982, pp. 3, 8, 10.

Rogers, A., & Magan, L. Directory of introductory psychology textbooks in print, 1982. *Teaching of Psychology,* 1982, *9,* 66–67.

Russo, N. F., & Malovich, N. J. Assessing the introductory psychology course. In J. M. Gappa & J. Pearce (Eds.), *Sex and gender in the social sciences: Reassessing the introductory course.* Washington, DC: American Psychological Association, 1982.

Russo, N., & O'Connell, A. Models from the past: Psychology's foremothers. *Psychology of Women Quarterly,* 1980, *5,* 11–54.

Sherif, C. W. Should there be a feminist methodology? *AWP Newsletter,* January–February 1982, pp. 3–4.

Sherman, J. Problem of sex differences in space perception and aspects of intellectual functioning. *Psychological Review,* 1967, *74,* 290–299.

Sherman, J. Field articulation, sex, spatial visualization, dependency, practice, laterality of the brain, and growth order. *Perceptual and Motor Skills,* 1974, *38,* 1223–1235.

Sherman, J. Rape: Psychological aspects. *Weekly Psychological Update.* Biomedia Inc., 1980, *1* (11).

Sidorowicz, L., & Lunney, G. S. Baby X revisited. *Sex Roles,* 1980, *6,* 67–74.

Spence, J. T., & Helmreich, R. L. *Masculinity and femininity.* Austin: University of Texas Press, 1978.

Stevens, G., & Gardner, S. *The Women of Psychology (Vols. 1 & 2).* Cambridge, MA: Schenkman Publishing Company, 1982.

Thomas, M. Carey. Women's college and university education. *Educational Review,* January 1908, pp. 64–85.

Thompson, C. *On women.* New York: Basic Books, 1964.

Tobias, S. Sexist equations. *Psychology Today,* January 1982, pp. 14–17.

Travers, J., & Milgram, S. An experimental study of the small world problem. *Sociometry,* 1969, *32,* 125–443.

Tresemer, D. The cumulative record of research on "fear of success," *Sex Roles*, 1976, *2*, 217–236.

Tresemer, D. (Ed.). *Fear of success.* New York: Plenum, 1977.

Unger, R. Sex as a social reality: Field and laboratory research. *Psychology of Women Quarterly*, 1981, *5*, 645–653.

Wallston, B. What are the questions in psychology of women? A feminist approach to research. *Psychology of Women Quarterly*, 1981, *5*, 597–617.

Walsh, M. R. *Doctors wanted: No women need apply.* New Haven: Yale University Press, 1977.

Watson, R. I. *The great psychologists.* Philadelphia: Lippincott, 1971.

Weissman, M. M., & Klerman, G. L. Sex differences and the epidemology of depression. In E. Howell & M. Bayes (Eds.), *Women and mental health.* New York: Basic Books, 1981.

Wilson, E. O. *Sociobiology: The new synthesis.* Cambridge, MA: Howard University Press, 1975.

Witkin, H. A., Birnbaum, J., Lomonaco, S., Lehr, S., & Hunan, J. L. Cognitive patterning in congenitally totally blind children. *Child Development*, 1968, *39*, 768–786.

Wolman, B. B. Between men and women. In R. K. Unger & F. L. Denmark (Eds.), *Women: Dependent or independent variable?* New York: Psychological Dimensions, 1975.

COMMENTS

Few would question Denmark's conviction that "students—females and males—deserve information about both women and men." Nor would many question that to provide this information requires an accurate presentation of a wide range of human experience, both female and male. Perhaps less agreement would occur, however, if one asked whether such information is already being provided in introductory psychology courses. How many instructors believe that they are failing to do so, even though they do not include material on the psychology of women in the course? Considering the latter question is crucial to the major purpose of this summary: How best to teach the psychology of women to students enrolled in introductory psychology courses.

How people think and act is influenced by social ideology, social norms, and social organization—and contemporary women and men still live in a largely patriarchal society. Denmark points out that sex-role socialization is as critical an influence on the personality development of women and men as observed sex-related differences in various achievement areas. Differential evaluation on the basis of sex is also well documented in the psychological literature. The male is rated higher than the equivalent female in such areas as task performance and leadership ability, for example. Differential evaluation of women and men not only influences decisions about ability and achievement, but also devalues female-related activities and topics. Some academic psychologists view the psychology of women as a collection of "women's issues" rather than as a legitimate area of research and teaching. Communicating this attitude to students, whether directly by stating opinions or indirectly by failing to discuss relevant subject matter within their own courses, may result in students' devaluing the subject matter.

Clearly instructors' attitudes and beliefs regarding women and men are a key factor in mainstreaming the psychology of women into introductory psychology courses. Instructors, many of whom were educated at a time when women were viewed quite differently in this society than they are today, need to be aware of how their personal views on the psychology of women may influence how they present and interpret material to students. Inviting colleagues or advanced students to particular lectures may enhance their sensitivity to possible bias. It is also helpful to include in course evaluations specific items directed to instructors' attitudes toward the rights and roles of women and men, stereotyping on the basis of sex.

A second important factor is resources. Denmark's lecture provides a wealth of information and details material to incorporate into six core areas of introductory psychology. Instructors also need to keep abreast of advances and relevant resources in the psychology of women. This, of course, requires that materials about the psychology of women be available in campus libraries and in the books and journals instructors purchase for personal and professional development. Instructors also need to feel confident that the texts they select for their courses provide an accurate and current view of the psychology of women and that periodicals, such as the *Annual Review of Psychology*, incorporate research on the psychology of women.

I return to my initial question of how best to teach material on the psychology of women to undergraduates. Again it is important that instructors and students remain aware of the social context and of the pervasive stereotypic views of men and women that still exist. Mastering the subject matter on the psychology of women would indeed be difficult if one held stereotypic views of women's attributes, behaviors, abilities, and roles. Thus one very important aspect of teaching is to use methods that allow students to examine their attitudes and belief systems about women and men and that foster discussions among students about their views. (Denmark includes references to a number of excellent exercises used successfully by instructors.) In addition, subject matter related to women's roles and status might be presented more effectively by male and female coteachers than by either a male or a female teacher alone. Coteaching might be particularly desirable in presenting topics such as sociobiology that convey to the state of being female or male greater stimulus value and thus may have greater influence on students' reactions.

Effectively incorporating the psychology of women into introductory psychology courses requires more than an understanding of a body of knowledge. Instructors must also be aware of both personal attitudes and institutional biases that may influence their own teaching and their students' learning.

IRWIN G. SARASON

CONTEMPORARY ABNORMAL PSYCHOLOGY: DEVELOPMENTS AND ISSUES

I rwin G. Sarason is a professor at the University of Washington. Since receiving his doctorate at Indiana University in 1955, he has conducted extensive research in the areas of personality, stress, and maladaptive behavior.

Sarason's research has been concerned with an interactional approach to personality, with special reference to the problems of anxiety and stress. He is currently studying the role of social support as a moderator of the effects of stressful life changes and the role of cognitive factors in the experience of anxiety.

Sarason's bibliography includes over 150 items, most of which are research reports. He is a co-author of *Psychology: The Frontiers of Behavior* and *Abnormal Psychology*. He is the editor of *Test Anxiety: Theory, Research and Applications* and co-editor of the *Stress and Anxiety* series.

Sarason is a fellow of the American Psychological Association and the American Association for the Advancement of Science and past president of the Western Psychology Association and Washington State Psychological Association. He has been a fellow at the Netherlands Institute for Advanced Study. He has been at the University of Washington for his entire career but has served as visiting professor at University College, London; University of Stockholm; University of Massachusetts; University of Hawaii; and University of Alaska.

IRWIN G. SARASON

CONTEMPORARY ABNORMAL PSYCHOLOGY: DEVELOPMENTS AND ISSUES

A bnormal psychology is concerned with maladjustment, ineffectiveness, unhappiness, and, in some cases, danger to self and others. This article is about some of the important developments and crosscurrents in the field. To attempt, in one article, a comprehensive review of all new evidence concerning the forms of behavior that have been labeled as abnormal would result in superficiality. To deal only with a few topics would be misleading. In deciding how to navigate between this Scylla and Charybdis, I have sought a reasonable compromise: to review comprehensively the theoretical perspectives that currently guide research and clinical practice and to give examples of some ways in which these perspectives have been applied. A major goal of the article is to provide instances illustrating how theories about the same phenomenon complement or sometimes infiltrate each other.

The article begins with a discussion of four traditional theoretical approaches, with particular reference to areas of rapproachment among them. I will also describe a multiperspective point of view that grows from the interactional perspective and from research on vulnerability to mental illness. Research in four clinical groups—depression, schizophrenia, anxiety disorders, and psychophysiological reactions—will be reviewed with special attention to theory and research relationships. Two new areas of concern to abnormal psychologists, behavioral medicine and health psychology, will be noted. The last major section of the article is a description and analysis of the *Diagnostic and Statistical Manual of Mental Disorders* (DSM III) of the American Psychiatric Association.

Theories of Abnormal Behavior

Theoretical perspectives serve as lenses, reflecting and shaping conceptions of human nature. They prod researchers and clinicians to ask certain kinds of questions. Although the diversity of theories in abnormal psychology is wide, four theoretical perspectives, one basically biological and three primarily psychological, are particularly influential at the present time. Each focuses attention on certain types of empirical relationships. The theories are (a) the biological perspective, which emphasizes the role of bodily processes; (b) the psychodynamic perspective, which emphasizes the roles of anxiety and inner conflict; (c) the learning perspective, which focuses attention on the influential role of the environment in the life of responsive organisms; and (d) the cognitive perspective, which looks to defective thinking and problem-solving as causes of behavioral abnormality. Although each of these perspectives deals with a piece of reality, the pieces are often quite different. Consequently, there is no reason to commit oneself to one particular theoretical position and feel called upon to explain all abnormal behavior in terms of its concepts. Theories often make differentially valuable contributions to the understanding of different types of problems. Further, with a topic as complex as abnormal behavior, it is a good idea to be wary of too simple an explanation of its occurrence. Because two of these approaches, those viewing behavior from the biological and cognitive perspectives, have been the focus of recent surges of both theoretical interest and research efforts, they will be discussed in somewhat more detail than the remaining pair.

Examples of the dangers of adopting too rigid a theoretical position are many. For example, the relatively high incidence of severe behavior disorders in old persons represents a major social problem for our aging population. A high percentage of these problems are related to bodily changes that are typically part of the aging process. However, it would be a mistake to say that psychotic behavior among old people is due simply to brain deterioration and disorders of the circulatory system. Two people with the same type of brain disorder might behave quite differently, depending upon their life histories, their concepts of themselves, and their worries about death and dying. The various theoretical perspectives are not equally applicable to the different types of personal maladaptation, and in any given case, clinicians would be well advised to assess the relevance of each to the problems with which they deal.

The Biological Perspective

This perspective became very popular in the eighteenth and nineteenth centuries. The great leaps forward in anatomy, physiology, and genetics made it seem reasonable that a biological cause might eventually be found for every disorder, physical or behavioral. Major impetus for the biological point of view came from findings about the relationship between bodily infections and defects on the one hand and disordered behavior on the other. Perhaps the most dramatic of these was the discovery in the nineteenth and early twentieth centuries of the link between syphilitic infection in early adulthood and general paresis, a serious deterioration of the brain that often followed when the person reached middle age.

Recent theorizing about the role of biological factors is, of course, based on more solid information than were the conjectures of the past. This information supports the argument that biological factors are important in some, but certainly not all, conditions. Modern advances in several areas of biology and medicine have continued to motivate researchers. For example, equipment and techniques such as the PET scan that allow understanding of brain activity patterns without surgery or other invasive procedures are beginning to permit previously inconceivable studies of brain-behavior relationships. On another dimension, research on heredity and genetics has led to the discovery that certain chromosomal defects are responsible for metabolic disorders, which in turn lead to specific forms of mental retardation such as Down's syndrome, and that certain recessive genes are responsible for metabolic disorders such as phenylketonuria (PKU). The list of behavioral problems in which biological processes play at least some role is lengthening, as is the list of biological therapies. It is increasingly recognized that maladaptive behavior is often a joint product of disordered processes in the body (for example, a hormonal deficiency), in psychological functioning (for example, a tendency toward shyness), and in the social environment (for example, a high unemployment rate in the community).

Two examples of problems studied from the biological perspective concern bodily responses to stress and identification of biological processes that may produce changes in disordered thought and behavior. Illustrative of the first type of problem is research on the bodily correlates of stress. The word stressor refers to a condition that increases the effort needed to achieve biological and psychological adaptation. Examples of stressors are disease germs and psychological experiences such as an insult or the turmoil of military combat. Hormones secreted by the endocrine system help to mobilize the physical resources of the organism either to fight or to escape the stressor's effects. The output of the endocrine glands is affected by stressors and direct nervous stimulation.

Illustrative of the second type of problem is research on the endorphins, often called the body's natural opiates. These neurochemicals produce their chemical effects by fitting into those sites, or receptors, that are specifically designed to accept them. Because the endorphins are chemically similar to opium and related substances, it seems that endorphins may offer a new way to understand the process of addiction. There are, of course, equally important environmental, psychosocial, and personality factors that influence the actual addictive behaviors. If scientists can create nonaddictive chemicals that function like the opiates, they may be able to ease pain of all kinds, including that connected with stopping a heroin habit. Before this can happen, much more information about the brain reward system and endorphins will be needed. Momentous as the discovery of endorphins was, it is not yet clear exactly what their functions are.

Although there is abundant evidence that various behavioral deficits result from bodily defects, many unanswered questions remain. Often the information available about possible organic factors is not sufficiently clear-cut to permit a high degree of certainty about the causes of abnormal behavior. For example, a person with memory losses and thought disturbances may have fallen on his or her head, but the actual effects of the fall on brain tissue may be by no means obvious. Clinicians find it necessary to exercise caution in weighing the relative importance of organic damage and psychological factors. Full understanding of the brain's role in abnormal behavior will require extensive research concerning the interrelationships of basic psychological and biological processes.

One of the most productive areas of biological research on abnormal behavior is psychopharmacology, which investigates the effects of drugs on behavior. During recent years various drugs have been used extensively in treating maladaptive behavior such as extreme anxiety, feelings of severe depression, hallucinations, or delusions. While the pill that will cure mental illness, like a process to turn metal into gold, has not been invented, great strides in biological therapies are being made. Antipsychotic, antianxiety, and antidepressant drugs are now often highly effective in reducing particular types of maladaptive behavior. These drugs, as well as narcotics (such as opium) and hallucinogens (such as LSD) influence perceptual, cognitive, and motor responses by blocking or modifying certain biochemical and physiological processes, particularly those involved in neural transmission in the brain. Unfortunately, designs in psychopharmacological research have often studied only drugs as independent variables. As a consequence, we do not know as much as we should about possible interactions among psychological, social, and pharmacological variables.

The Psychodynamic Perspective

Psychodynamic approaches to behavior assume that, in varying degrees, observable behavior (overt responses) is a function of intrapsychic processes (covert events). Not all psychodynamic theorists emphasize the same inner events and sources of environmental stimulation, but they do agree that personality is shaped by a combination of inner and outer events, with emphasis on the inner ones.

Because thoughts and feelings are not directly observable, psychodynamic theorists infer them from overt behavior and use their inferences to explain other aspects of overt behavior. Apart from the contribution psychodynamic theories have made to our understanding of human behavior, they have been influential because they are the systems out of which psychotherapy developed. While clinical psychoanalysis as developed by Freud is an infrequently used form of treatment today, its basic elements and theory of mental events have greatly influenced the development of the entire field of psychotherapy. Central to Freud's and several other psychodynamic theories is the concept of anxiety. Freud defined anxiety as a response to perceived danger or stress. He distinguished between two kinds of anxiety-provoking situations. In one, of which birth might be the prototype, anxiety is caused by excessive external stimulation that the organism does not have the capacity to handle. In the other, Freud assumed that when inhibitions and taboos prevent the constructive expression of psychic energy, the excessive internal stimulation can result in anxiety.

Anxiety often arises in anticipation of danger rather than after a dangerous situation occurs. Anxiety, like physical pain, thus serves a protective function by signaling the approach of danger and warning us to prepare our defenses. But anxiety can also indicate an inability to cope with personal threat and danger. The meaning of anxiety is a central problem to be understood during psychoanalysis. A later portion of this essay deals with the current state of knowledge concerning the anxiety disorders, conditions in which anxiety plays a prominent role.

The Learning Perspective

Learning psychologists view behavior as a product of stimulus-response (S-R) relationships. Both the psychodynamic and the learning approaches to behavior are deterministic, but the nature of determinism is quite different in the two orientations. Learning psychologists use stimulus-response principles rather than intrapsychic events to account for behavioral development. To change behavior, learning psychologists concentrate on changing relevant aspects of the environment, particularly sources of reinforcement. Classical and operant conditioning and observational learning have provided the basis for many behavior therapy techniques.

Although orthodox behaviorists continue to believe that covert events such as thoughts and feelings do not count in the study of maladaptation because they cannot be directly observed and measured, many learning theorists now emphasize the role of mediational processes in the acquisition of abnormal behavior. Learning theorists have often described people as being more or less at the mercy of the environment, whereas in recent years the relationship between the individual and the environment has come to be seen as reciprocal, as a two-way street. For example, while the social environment influences the depressed person, he or she also significantly influences the environment.

The Cognitive Perspective

The cognitive like the psychodynamic perspective is concerned with internal processes. But rather than stress urges, needs, and motivations, it emphasizes how people acquire and interpret information and use it in solving problems of life. Typically, the cognitive perspective has paid more attention to present thoughts and problem-solving strategies than to personal histories. However, histories of cognition are now receiving some attention (Sarason, 1979). The relationships among emotions, motivations, and cognitive processes are also receiving increasing study. Overlap between the cognitive perspective and other approaches such as the psychoanalytic is becoming more evident (Bieber, 1980).

Dollard and Miller (1950) were among the first to see the common threads that run through the psychodynamic, learning, and cognitive theories. They pointed out the similarity between the reinforcement principle and Freud's pleasure principle and also made use of cognitive concepts by describing maladaptive behavior as the joint product of unfortunate life experiences and maladaptive thinking. They viewed insight into the roots of one's behavior as the acquisition of self-awareness responses and used the term "learning dilemma" to refer to situations that necessitate this sort of revision. Despite their preference for describing behavior in terms of habits and learning, they emphasized the individual's cognitive resolution of learning dilemmas and of conflicts in general.

Interactional Approach to Abnormal Psychology

In a high percentage of cases, the variables emphasized by the different theoretical perspectives interact—that is, they exert joint effects. An old person with an impaired blood supply to the brain who happens to be living in a happy social setting and has always been quite adaptable might not be seriously hampered by the inevitable memory lapses that occur when portions of the brain are temporarily starved for blood. A less adaptable person with the same affliction forced to live in an impersonal nursing home might become completely disorganized by increased feelings of stress and might die prematurely. The interactional view of abnormal behavior recognizes the contributions of the variables emphasized in the various traditional theoretical perspectives and directs attention to their joint effects or interactions. Abnormal behavior can result from any or all of a large number of factors.

An interactional perspective focuses attention on level of adaptation as a function of both personal characteristics and situational factors. Personal characteristics include vulnerabilities (a physical handicap or a low threshold for getting angry) and strengths (cognitive skills or social awareness). Situational factors include both environmental demands and constraints and buffering factors such as social support. Stress, which is involved in many forms of disordered behavior, arises when an individual is faced with the need to deal with a challenging situation in the absence of an adequate repertory of coping responses.

There is evidence that in some situations social support serves as a protection against stress and as a condition conducive to the acquisition and use of effective coping skills. While the mechanism by which close social relationships are protective has yet to be worked out, the following factors are probably involved: a sense of intimacy, a perception of social integration through shared social concerns, a reassurance of worth, the opportunity to be nurtured by others, a sense of reliable alliance, and guidance. Knowing that other people are confronting similar life stresses and sharing upsetting feelings and thoughts with them are often very beneficial. Too often the person in a crisis seems to hide or withdraw and thus becomes deprived of these opportunities for social support. Special group programs for persons undergoing intense or prolonged stress offer one method of counteracting this withdrawal tendency and thereby providing social supports that facilitate the strengthening of participants' coping skills (Cowen, 1982; Pilisuk, 1982).

Theoretical Perspectives
and Their Influence on Research

Keeping this sketch of theoretical perspectives in mind, let me examine some specific types of abnormal behavior in order to illustrate how they have been conceptualized, describe current research relevant to each, and point out examples of interactions that have been identified among the variables employed by the different theories.

Depression

The term depression is used in everyday language to refer to a feeling state, a reaction to a situation, or a person's characteristic style of behavior. The simple feeling of depression is usually known as "the blues." It may occur in rainy weather, during an annoying cold, or after an argument with a friend. Often an event that is usually expected to be happy ends with such blue feelings. People may experience the blues after holidays such as Christmas or New Year's Day, after moving to a new home, or following childbirth. Feelings of depression stemming from holidays, new housing, or a change in school or job usually fade away quickly after the event has passed or the person becomes accustomed to the new surroundings. For most people, these situations seem to represent only a temporary, nonincapacitating sadness that disappears when the situation changes.

Another kind of depression is the grief or bereavement reaction, a sadness that comes from a death in the family or the disappointment that accompanies the end of a love affair. After the death of a significant person, most survivors experience what is usually called grief. This is entirely normal. In fact, not showing a mourning reaction might be bad for the person in the long run. Common features of grief include physical distress such as sighing, tightness of the throat, an empty feeling in the abdomen, and a feeling of muscular weakness. In addition, there may be preoccupation with the visual image of the dead person, guilt, and hostile reactions. During the process of grieving, the guilt, hostility, feelings of loss, and physical symptoms gradually disappear.

Because feelings of depression have been experienced by almost everyone, these feelings alone are not enough to call for a diagnosis of depression. Where does "normal" depression end and "clinical" depression begin? Some researchers believe that depression can be studied on a continuum from the blues of normality through the severe clinical categories (Blatt, D'Afflitti, & Quinlan, 1976). Others think that the blues and depression are two very different things (Akiskal,

1981). Unlike its effect on the blues, reassurance or helpful advice from friends or family is not enough to send depression away.

Feeling or mood alone does not distinguish the blues from depression because both are characterized by sadness. Clinical depression is much less common and a more serious problem of maladaptive behavior than the temporary blues we all feel once in a while. Yet clinical depression is perhaps the most frequent problem confronted by those who deal with the psychological problems of individuals. Among patients who see a physician for a physical complaint, at least 18 percent are also depressed, one third of them moderately or severely (Nielsen & Williams, 1980). For hospitalized patients in mental institutions, depression is also one of the most commonly diagnosed conditions (National Center for Health Statistics, 1980).

The cause of depression has been investigated from many of the major theoretical viewpoints. The most popular view at present is that there are distinct groups of depressives whose symptoms have different causes. The bipolar group, those who have episodes of both manic and depressive behaviors, are thought to have a strong genetic component to their disorder. In the unipolar group, depression occurs alone without manic episodes. Many researchers think that the unipolar category includes at least two subgroups. Individuals in the first subgroup may have become depressed as a result of an inability to cope with a difficult life situation. In the second subgroup, depression may be due to problems in neural transmission caused by the unavailability of a sufficient amount of the chemical transmitters called catecholamines. This chemical lack may be of genetic origin.

As is usually the case, the different theoretical approaches to depression have produced different types of studies and different data, all of which may have something to add to the complex problem of the disorder's causes and treatment.

Biological Approaches

Biological theories assume that the cause of depression lies in a biological malfunction that may or may not have an inherited base.

A major area of research in depression concerns the role of neurotransmitters. Some theorists have related depression to low levels of catecholamines, especially norepinephrine. Research has suggested that norepinephrine is related to mood changes, measurable feelings, and feelings of depression. For a number of years, the dominant view was the catecholamine theory of depression, which stresses the deficiency of available neurotransmitter chemicals (Schildkraut, 1965). Research now suggests that rather than the amount of catecholamines available, it may be problems in reception of the catecholamines by the receiving neuron that is important (Sulser, 1979).

For many people, low levels of norepinephrine excretion are found in periods of depression and high levels are found during mania. Evidence for this comes from monitoring norepinephrine levels in blood, urine, and cerebrospinal fluid. Another catecholamine, dopamine, has also been related to depression. Dopamine is associated with neuron groups related to coordination, regulation of foods and fluids, the effects of the hypothalamus on the pituitary gland, and the expression of emotion. Other researchers have linked depression to yet another neurotransmitter, serotonin. One problem in measuring any neurotransmitter action is that such measurements are not direct reflections of brain levels of the neurotransmitters. Neurotransmitters are produced not only in the brain but also in other parts of the nervous system and are involved in a number of body processes. In addition, measurement is difficult because neurotransmitters are very unstable compounds that rapidly change their chemical form.

Much of the understanding of the role of neurotransmitters has come about through observations of the effects of drugs administered to patients, sometimes in an attempt to treat other disorders. For example, reserpine, one of the early tranquilizing drugs used in the treatment of high blood pressure or hypertension, was observed to cause depression in humans, sometimes serious enough to require hospitalization. Reserpine was known to cause depletion of some chemicals in the catecholamine group that are necessary in nerve impulse transmission. This suggested to scientists a relationship between neurotransmitters and depression. The two drug groups now most often used to treat depression are the tricyclics and the monoamine oxidase (MAO) inhibitors. The first tricyclic, imipramine, was originally used to treat schizophrenia. Researchers observed that while it did not have the intended effect, it did lessen depressed feelings of the patient. The first MAO inhibitor, iproniazid, was originally used to treat tuberculosis and was found to produce elated moods in the TB patients. On the basis of these clues, researchers turned their attention to the effects of drugs of the tricyclic and MAO inhibitor families in the treatment of depression.

The tricyclics and the MAO inhibitors produce their effects in somewhat different ways. MAO inhibitors retard the breakdown of norepinephrine so that it remains active longer. The tricyclic drugs increase available norepinephrine in another way. They slow its reabsorption by the transmitter neuron and thus keep more available in the synapse. Which group of drugs and which particular drug within a category is found to be effective for a particular individual is still usually a result of trial and error by the physician. Usually, one of the tricyclic drugs is preferred because the MAO inhibitors have more potentially dangerous side effects. They also require stricter supervision of use because when combined with foods containing a substance called tyramine they may produce a toxic reaction and cause blood pressure to rise to a potentially life-threatening level. Since many common foods including cheese, chocolate, sour cream, and wine contain tyramine, use of MAO inhibitors requires careful dietary monitoring.

One of the problems in treatment of a severe episode of depression with either tricyclics or MAO inhibitors is the time lag between the beginning of their use and improvement of the depressed mood. Several weeks of administration may be required before an improvement is seen. If there is concern about suicide, a wait of three weeks or so may seem too great a risk. In such situations, or if drugs are not effective, electro-convulsive therapy (ECT) may be the treatment of choice because it produces a much more rapid effect. Electro-convulsive therapy involves passing a current of between 70 to 130 volts through a patient's head. After administering an anesthetic and a muscle relaxant, the current is administered through electrodes placed on one or both sides of the head. The muscle relaxant is given to prevent injury from the convulsion caused by the electric charge. Although ECT has many critics who fear it may cause brain damage and permanent memory loss, a recent assessment of its effects have given it a relatively clean bill of health (Scovern & Kilman, 1980). Most memory loss that is experienced fades rather quickly. Improved technology has also made the procedure safer. Placement of both the electrodes on one side of the head is now preferred because this procedure seems to reduce chance of memory loss.

Since most researchers agree that not all depressions have similar causes, an important task is to identify subgroups of depressed patients that have similar characteristics. Identification of homogeneous subgroups would not only make it easier to understand the causes of depression but even more important, might give clues that would cut down the number of trial and error attempts to find the most effective treatment for a particular individual.

One example of a biological approach to this classification task is the Dexamethasone Suppression Test (Carroll et al., 1981). Patients are given the steroid, dexamethasone. This chemical suppresses the production of cortisol, a hormone produced in the cortex of the brain. Normally this steroid should suppress the level of cortisol in the blood for about 24 hours. In some depressed patients, however, the suppression doesn't last that long. It is thought that this group may differ from other depressed people in additional ways, for example, be more likely to have family members who are depressed.

Another biological tool for separating depressed individuals into more homogeneous types is based on the study of periods of rapid eye movement (REM) sleep. One characteristic in some depressed individuals is a shortened period between falling asleep and the beginning of the first REM period (Kupfer, Foster, Coble, McPartland, & Ulrich, 1978). This also suggests some differences in physiological function. At first, interest in REM pattern in depressives was in the search for a method to differentiate types of depression as in the case of the Dexamethasone Suppression Test. However,the REM research also has significance for therapy. Depriving depressed individuals of REM sleep can help decrease their depression (Vogel, Vogel, McAbee, & Thurmond, 1980). This can be done simply by waking the sleeping individuals whenever REM occurs. This treatment seems to work on the same group of patients that is helped by tricyclic drugs. Vogel and his co-workers have suggested that perhaps tricyclic drugs also work by reducing REM sleep.

Psychological Approaches

Valuable research on depression has been carried out from psycho-dynamic, learning, and cognitive points of view.

In answering the question of why some individuals react to stress with irrational grief, most psychodynamic formulations focus on the history of relationships between the individual and the figure he or she was most dependent on as a child, usually the mother. Thus, an historical antecedent of depression is a disturbance in early childhood relationships. The disturbance might be the actual loss or a feared or fantasized loss of a parental figure. Because of its anxiety-provoking quality, this early loss is pushed out of awareness. Nevertheless, it exerts its influence and culminates in actual depression when set off by a symbolically significant event. Psychodynamic theories empha-size unconscious feelings and reactions to new situations based on what has happened earlier in life.

The importance of parental loss has been studied intensively in animal experiments. Research by Harry Harlow and others using monkeys has tested the effects on the infant of removal from the mother (Harlow & Suomi, 1974). At first, the typical infant shows agitation; this gradually changes to social withdrawal, slow responses to stimuli, and slow movement. Eventually, the baby assumes a col-lapsed self-clasping position that suggests behavior of someone who is severely depressed. Separation from their mothers also seems to make monkeys more likely to become depressed in later life if the level of stress becomes high.

Bowlby (1980), is one of the more prominent proponents of im-portance of loss or separation in childhood in later development. He thinks that separation of a child from its mother or other important figure during early childhood because of illness, travel, or other rea-sons, creates feelings of sadness, anger, and continuing anxiety that may affect emotional relationships in adult life. Several researchers have provided data that connect the probability of depression in adults with early experiences of loss. For example, Brown, Harris, and Copeland's (1977) survey of 459 women living in London found that women who had lost their mothers before the age of eleven had a greater risk of depression than other women. In addition, the most severe cases of depression were found in women who had experienced a death in the family before reaching age seventeen. While not everyone thinks that early loss has been definitely established as a factor increasing the risk of later depression (Crook & Eliot, 1980), it remains an important part of the psychodynamic perspective and the available evidence certainly suggests the need to study further the effects of early separation and loss.

Learning approaches have emphasized the relationship between lack of reinforcement and depression. The lack of reinforcement may have several causes. The environment may be generally nonreinforcing or even punishing, so responses are discouraged because they either receive no reinforcement or bring forth an unpleasant or punishing response from others. Peter Lewinsohn and his coworkers have been among the leaders in research on depression from the learning perspective. In general they emphasize that the low rate of behavior output and the feelings of sadness or unhappiness that we associate with depression are due to a low rate of positive reinforcement or a high rate of unpleasant experience.

This situation might come about for one or more of several reasons. It may be that few reinforcements or many punishing factors exist in the environment; the environment itself may be the problem. The person may lack social skills either to attract positive reinforcements or to cope effectively with unpleasant aversive events. For some reason reinforcements may seem less positive or punishments more negative to people prone to depression than to the average person; this may begin a cycle of decreased behavior or withdrawal that leads to fewer reinforcements or more punishments.

Depressed people experience a higher occurrence of unpleasant events in their lives and they also perceive these events as more unpleasant than do nondepressed people (Lewinsohn & Talkington, 1979). This greater negative response has been demonstrated not only by asking people to rate unpleasant events but also by behavior in a laboratory situation. For example, the autonomic responsiveness of depressed and nondepressed groups was compared following aversive stimulation in the form of mild electric shocks (Lewinsohn, Lobitz, & Wilson, 1973). The depressed group responded more (higher skin reactions) to the aversive stimuli than the nondepressed group did. This greater responsiveness might reasonably lead one to expect the depressed individual to show a greater-than-usual tendency to withdraw from situations that he or she found unpleasant. However, this withdrawal would also have the effect of decreasing the depressed person's chances for reinforcement. Once a person has become depressed, Lewinsohn believes, the depression is maintained because other people find depressed people unpleasant to be with. Acquaintances tend to avoid the depressive as much as possible and thus further decrease the person's rate of reinforcement, in effect intensifying the depression.

In treating clients who are depressed, Lewinsohn and his coworkers first strive to pinpoint specific person-environment interactions and events that are related to the depression. One step in doing this is to make home observations as part of the initial assessment (Lewinsohn & Arconad, 1981). This accomplishes several things. It alerts the client to the idea that depression is related to interactions with other people and with the environment and it also gives the therapist a productive and relatively unbiased way of learning about the behavior of the client and spouse or children or others in the environment. Other tools used in learning-based treatment are lists of pleasant and unpleasant events. The client lists events that might occur and how pleasant or unpleasant each was or would be if it happened. A tailor-made list is constructed to be used for daily recording of event occurrence. From this list the reinforcing value of each day's events can be easily computed. In addition the client rates his or her mood each day. This allows both the client and therapist to become aware of the relationship of mood and events for the client. In addition to this daily monitoring a specific treatment plan is prepared that includes training in those skills that the initial evaluation has shown to be lacking. This could include such things as assertion training, effective parenting, time management, and relaxation training.

The popularity of cognitive approaches to depression has increased greatly in recent years. Perhaps one reason for this is the obvious fact that the same event may affect two people very differently. Part of this difference may be due to the way each thinks about the event, to the cognitions each has. Aaron Beck's cognitive theory of depression has been influential in developing treatment procedures and has stimulated a great deal of research.

Beck (1967; Beck, Rush, Shaw, & Emery, Note 1) believes that depressed people are depressed because they have erroneous and exaggerated ways of thinking. The depressed person has a negative view of him- or herself, the world, and the future. Beck thinks these negative cognitions cause the depressed state, not the other way around. It is possible for depressive episodes to be precipitated by an external event, but it's what the individual thinks about it, rather than the event itself, that is the depression-producing factor.

Not only does the depression-prone person overgeneralize, he or she also tends to magnify personal faults and minimize positive personal qualities. Another problem is inexact labeling. The depressed person labels a situation as bad and then responds only to these distorted labels and not to the actual situation. In addition, Beck thinks that depressed people tend to compare themselves with others, which further lowers their self-esteem.

Why do these misperceptions come about? The depressed person sees him- or herself as a "loser," a misfit, destined always to get the short end of any deal and deserving no better. Beck's idea is that sense of loss, often the result of unrealistically high goals and expectations, is the primary factor. The depressed individual either misinterprets or exaggerates the loss or allocates overgeneralized, extravagant meanings to it.

Beck's ideas have stimulated a great deal of research both in laboratory studies and with groups of clinically depressed people. For example, in one study of memory, a series of adjectives were shown to three groups of women, a clinically depressed group, a group with psychotic diagnoses other than depression, and a nondepressed nonpatient control group (Derry & Kuiper, 1981). Some of the adjectives had depressed content, some did not. Each subject was asked to say whether or not each word described her. Later, when the subjects were asked to remember the words, the depressed group remembered those adjectives they had selected with depressed content; this was not true of the nondepressed groups.

Another idea that plays a role in cognitive theories of depression is helplessness. It has been argued that people who are depressed feel helpless to control their environment. No matter what they do they think they will be unable to affect the way things turn out. It is possible that some people learn to be helpless because of what they had learned in the past about their ability to change certain situations. Martin Seligman (1974, 1975) first popularized the idea of learned helplessness based on learning theory principles. He found that dogs who had earlier been exposed to electric shock that they could not escape did not learn to avoid shock in a later experiment. In contrast, dogs that had not been shocked earlier learned shock avoidance quickly.

According to the original helplessness theory, at least one type of depression is caused by the expectation that the response and the outcome are not related. Depression results not from feelings of inadequacy but because in some situations people believe no possible behavior can control the outcome. For example, 75 percent of the teachers in a study in the Los Angeles school system described their personal level of stress at school as at least moderate and 20 percent said their stress level was almost unbearable (Hammen & deMayo, 1982). Of the 75 teachers, 15 reported symptoms as severe as those of depressed individuals in psychotherapy, yet unlike many depressed persons these teachers did not describe their inadequacies as a cause of their stress. Instead they saw the situation as one in which neither they nor other teachers could possibly have control.

The original learned helplessness theory had a tremendous influence on psychological research, and like most theories it was found that it did not explain all the experimental results (Miller & Norman, 1979). Seligman and his co-workers have revised the theory to take account of the experimental findings the first helplessness theory had stimulated. The revised helplessness theory stresses the importance of cognitions, specifically the attributions people make in a situation, in determining whether they will become depressed (Abramson, Seligman, & Teasdale, 1978). According to the revised helplessness theory, depression is more likely in people who attribute negative qualities to themselves as a result of experiencing situations in which they feel helpless. There are three dimensions to these feelings of helplessness. The first has to do with whether the person sees the problem as external or internal. People are more likely to become depressed or to have a low self-image if they attribute the situation to their personal inability to control outcomes. Such a person sees himself or herself as the only one who can't cope with the problem. This is quite different from those, such as some of the teachers in Los Angeles, who feel that anyone in their situation would have a hard time. The second dimension has to do with the global-specific continuum. If an individual sees what happens as proof of being totally helpless, he or she is more likely to be depressed than someone who feels helpless only in a particular situation. The third dimension has to do with whether the situation is viewed as stable (chronic) or unstable (acute). People who think their helplessness will go on for years are more likely to be depressed than those who think it will just last a short time. Thus, what began as a learning theory in its original conception is now clearly cognitive in its emphasis.

The theories of both Beck and Seligman have been important in creating a great deal of enthusiasm for the cognitive approach, both in understanding how depressed and nondepressed people differ and in exploring how understanding these differences can make therapy more effective. The two researchers developed their theories in very different ways. Beck used his observations of the thinking of clinical clients as a basis for his theory. Seligman used his observation of animals in more controllable experimental situations as an analogue for human behavior and later extended his work to human beings. Each approach has advantages. The two theories have many things in common but they differ in Beck's emphasis on a depressed person's negative self-image and Seligman's emphasis on perceived control.

Both Beck's theory and the revised learned helplessness hypothesis stress the inaccuracy of self-perception in depression, yet in a paradox, experimenters studying how well people assessed their own social competence found that depressed patients were quite realistic about their own social skills. In contrast, other psychotic patients and also normal control subjects tended to see themselves as more competent than other people saw them. Even more interesting, the depressed patient's realistic self-image tended to become less realistic as therapy progressed. As they became less depressed, the patients became less realistic about their effect on others. In short, they deluded themselves more in the way that nonpatients do (Lewinsohn, Mischel, Chaplin, & Barton, 1980).

This fits in very well with an observation made by Freud:

> When in his (the depressive's) heightened self-criticism he describes himself as petty, egoistic, dishonest, lacking in independence, one whose sole aim has been to hide the weakness of his own nature, it may be, so far as we know, that he has come pretty near to understanding himself; we only wonder why a man has to be ill before he can be accessible to a truth of this kind. (Freud, 1917/1957, p. 246)

The crucial question then becomes whether depression leads people to become more realistic or whether realistic people are more vulnerable, thus more likely to become depressed. As yet research has not unravelled this puzzle.

This review of the psychological theories of depression illustrates their common threads as much as their differences. The major psychological theories of depression seem to compete with each other only if we ignore the growing areas of overlap that recent research has highlighted. For example, Lewinsohn's learning approach and Beck's cognitive theory of depression started out quite differently. However, as the learning approach has developed an emphasis on social reinforcement and in some cases more emphasis on attribution, and as Beck has included such items as a behavioral checklist of events and moods, many of the therapeutic techniques have become similar. Seligman's theory of learned helplessness also started out as a rather conventional learning theory, but the revised theory with its emphasis on causal attribution now also overlaps considerably with Beck's ideas. Psychodynamic theorists and therapists also increasingly stress cognitive distortions; however, they tend to focus not only on how these affect present behavior but where they came from in the client's earlier life.

Today the various psychological and biological theories seem competitive with each other primarily because they involve the manipulation of different independent and dependent variables. As research designs become more sophisticated and incorporate a greater variety of variables, the illusion of clearly demarcated differences may become less apparent.

Schizophrenia

What causes schizophrenic behavior is not known. It seems likely that it is produced by the interaction of a number of different factors under particular kinds of conditions. Questions dealing with schizophrenic behavior have been investigated from many points of view. Experimental manipulation and naturalistic, observational research have both been used in attempts to determine in what ways those people who show schizophrenic behavior differ from those who do not, in such characteristics as heredity, family structure, or biochemistry. As we saw with regard to depression, the focus of much schizophrenia research originates in the theoretical views held by the researchers.

Biological Approaches

There is some evidence suggesting that schizophrenics may be biologically different from other people. Viewing this problem from the biological perspective leads to two different kinds of questions. The first major question is whether it can be shown that there is a heredity factor in schizophrenia. If such a factor exists, and most people agree that it does, then what hereditary mechanisms are involved? The second major question is: What specific biological factors can be found that distinguish between people who show schizophrenic behavior and people who don't? If these differences can be identified they may lead to clues about the mechanisms that cause schizophrenic behavior.

The risk of schizophrenia is definitely greater for someone whose relatives show schizophrenic behavior than for someone who does not have such relatives. This fact has been established for a long time. However, knowing just that much does not definitely establish a hereditary factor. It could be that merely living with a schizophrenic parent or sibling could create a stressful environment conducive to schizophrenic behavior. Researchers have struggled with this question for a long time and have by means of twin, family, and adoption studies, established quite clearly that there is a hereditary risk factor in schizophrenia (Kessler, 1981).

There are also strong arguments for the assumption that biochemical factors play a role in at least some types of schizophrenias. One impetus to a search for biochemical clues is the effectiveness of some antipsychotic drugs that are known to produce certain biochemical changes. Finding biochemical or other organic differences between schizophrenics and control subjects is not difficult. The problem lies in finding an explanation that takes account of all the possibilities that might cause a particular result. One difficulty has been poor experimental designs. Often the control group lives under very different conditions from the patient group. For example, schizophrenics who have been hospitalized for many years lead sedentary lives, eat a routine hospital diet, and have been treated with various drugs; they may be under constant stress, which has been shown to cause biological changes. The control group, on the other hand, may consist of college students, hospital nurses, or nonprofessional employees, whose lives will obviously differ from the lives of the patients in many ways. Any experimental findings may simply reflect these differences.

Recent research reflects a new and much more sophisticated approach to biological differences. Instead of looking for some abnormal substance unique to schizophrenics, interest is now centered in looking for abnormalities in biochemical functioning. Because of development of new and increasingly sensitive biological techniques and the discovery of new neurochemical systems in the body, this research promises to be more productive than past efforts. Although the techniques for dealing with unstable, rapidly changing chemical compounds still are not adequate and many experimental findings cannot be reproduced by other investigators, progress has been made.

Just as neurotransmitters are currently thought to be important in at least some types of affective disorders, biologically oriented research in schizophrenia also stresses the importance of their function. In the affective disorders, research is centered on norepinephrine; in schizophrenia, current research has been focused on dopamine. The idea that dopamine is involved comes from two sources. One is the finding that the drug amphetamine given in large doses is capable of producing behavior very similar to that of paranoid schizophrenia in individuals without any history of psychological difficulties. Even more important, low doses of amphetamines made some symptoms worse in individuals who had schizophrenic disorder. Biochemically, amphetamines increase the amount of the catecholamines, dopamine, and norepinephrine available at the synapse. The dopamine theory, simply stated, says that there is an excess of dopamine at certain synapses in the brain. This is thought to be due either to an excess production of dopamine or to faulty regulation of the feedback apparatus by which the dopamine returns and is stored by vesicles in the presynaptic neuron. However, it might also be due to oversensitive dopamine receptors or too great a number of receptors.

It may be that antipsychotic drugs work by locking into the dopamine receptors so that they are blocked. The story cannot be as simple as this, because antipsychotic drugs typically produce, not a quick behavioral improvement, but rather a gradual improvement over about a six-week period. This time lag cannot be handled by the present dopamine hypothesis. However, like any good hypothesis, the dopamine hypothesis has made investigators aware of many more questions and generated a great deal of research. Despite its deficiencies it is still the dominant biochemical theory of schizophrenia. At the same time, researchers are looking at other biochemical relationships. For example, studies of platelet monoamine oxidase (MAO) show there may be a relationship between decreased MAO activity and chronic schizophrenia (Wyatt, Potkin, & Murphy, 1979).

A developing field of research in the biochemistry of schizophrenia centers on the role of opiate receptors and opiate-like peptides or endorphins in the brain in producing schizophrenic behavior. It is not clear whether the endorphins act to improve or worsen psychotic symptoms (Bowers, 1981). However, it seems likely that endorphins play a role in the body's synthesis of dopamine. Some researchers believe that the endorphins may alter the catecholamines or be altered by them. Others think they may play an independent role in psychosis.

Time and continued research will determine whether the current concentration of interest in schizophrenia as a chemically produced disorder will yield important insights into the cause of the disorder. Whether this avenue of research proves fruitful or not, it is certain that, at present, a great deal of attention is focused on the role of these biochemicals in psychotic behavior. Just as in the case of the affective disorders, biochemical studies on living human beings are difficult to carry out because of the indirect measurements required. Although researchers want to study the biochemical changes going on in the brain, they are forced to infer these changes by indirect measurements using blood, urine, or cerebrospinal fluid as the source of data. Clearly a great deal can happen biochemically between the brain's production of chemicals and their analysis. Another difficulty is that some of these chemicals are also produced elsewhere in the body and there is no way to determine their source in the analysis.

Psychological Approaches

From a learning point of view, the distinctive feature of schizophrenia is the extinction or lack of development of conventional responses to social stimuli. Accompanying the social impoverishment is a highly personalized response repertory that, regardless of how unusual it is, has been learned in basically the same way as conventional responses. For the learning psychologist, rehabilitating the schizophrenic requires control over the reinforcements that are related to the development of these unusual responses.

Can a learning approach explain why a schizophrenic hallucinates? What is reinforcing about a hallucination? There are no ready answers to these complex questions. Because individuals are deprived or have deprived themselves of the rewards of meaningful social relationships, their hallucinations may have taken on considerable stimulus value. Other people can hurt the schizophrenic, but hallucinations are safe. In their early stages, bizarre responses such as hallucinations may be difficult to distinguish from nonhallucinatory activities and may easily be unwittingly reinforced. Thus, from an operant conditioning standpoint, to modify the bizarre behavior of the schizophrenic it is necessary to modify these existing reinforcement patterns. This may require a drastic overhaul of the patient's environment. Bizarre behavior that was previously reinforced (usually unwittingly) must no longer be responded to in a positive manner.

At present the main focus of the learning perspective in dealing with schizophrenia in individuals is to increase their interaction with other people by helping them develop social skills and overcome anxiety in social situations. Token economies and social skills training have been included in many rehabilitation programs.

From a psychodynamic perspective, the irrational thought and bizarre behavior of the schizophrenic are caused by a consciousness of urges and ideas that remain inaccessible to most individuals. The first clear signs of the schizophrenic's bizarre behavior or acute withdrawal are usually toward the end of adolescence. According to most psychodynamic formulations, the onset of symptoms does not represent a new problem but rather indicates a life crisis in which previously controlled thoughts and fantasies are given overt expression. The maladaptive behavior becomes noticeable during the postadolescent period, because at that time the individual is expected to carve an independent niche in life. Although a child can retreat into a fantasy world, adults are expected to fend for themselves. Schizophrenic postadolescents have no faith in their ability to accomplish anything of value in the real world. Thus, they deal with these new challenges by focusing on the safety of inner stimuli. Researchers interested in how thought, feelings, and interpersonal relationships may be related to the development of schizophrenic behavior have concentrated on the areas of family relationships and communication among family members.

A number of studies suggest that a negative emotional relationship may exist in families in which a child later becomes schizophrenic or shows disordered behavior that in some ways suggests schizophrenia. This idea, once very popular, is currently out of favor and such concepts as the schizophrenogenic mother, for example, are no longer viable. However, in an effort to improve on the methodological deficiencies of the older studies, two new long-term studies at the University of Rochester and at the University of California at Los Angeles are looking into parent-child relations in high-risk families. In one study (part of the UCLA project), whether the parents showed genuine concern for the child or expressed criticism in a laboratory test was a predictor of the child's diagnosis five years later. Parents of children with schizophrenic-like problems tended to be more critical, intrusive, and guilt-inducing than parents whose children did not display such behavior in adolescence (Doane, West, Goldstein, Rodnick, & Jones, 1981).

Of all aspects of family life, disordered communication among family members seems the most likely to be associated with the development of schizophrenia. Probably the most extensive work on communication deviance has been carried out by Wynne and Singer and their colleagues (Wynne, Singer, Bartko, & Toohey, 1977). The major way they have assessed parental communication is through the use of the Rorschach test. In general, children who were schizophrenic came from families where both parents have high deviance scores. Although most researchers agree that there is some deviant communication in families with a schizophrenic child, there are still many questions to be answered. Is the parent's deviance a causal factor in the child's unusual characteristics, problems of attention, thinking patterns, and so on, or are these characteristics a cause of the parent's behavior? The answers are still not clear.

Since thought disorder is one of the defining characteristics of schizophrenia, the cognitive perspective should be particularly applicable. A great deal of research has been focused on the cognitive functioning of schizophrenics. In attempts to distinguish between schizophrenics and normals, researchers have looked for differences in attention, perception, language, memory processes, category formation, and reasoning.

Disordered thinking is not unique to schizophrenia. Disordered thinking is part of the same continuum with normal thinking, not something completely different. In one study a number of groups were compared by tape-recording all their verbalizations on an intelligence test (the Wechsler Adult Intelligence Scale) and a personality test (the Rorschach). The responses were all rated on a thought disorder index that weighs thought slippage in terms of severity. Mild peculiar responses were given a low weight, looseness of associations and queer responses a moderate weight, and confusion and other serious disturbances a high weight. Although schizophrenics had the highest score, no group was free of some thought disorder. Of special interest was the finding that parents of schizophrenic patients showed more thought disorder than parents of nonschizophrenic patients (Johnson & Holzman, in press). Such a measure of thought disorder could also be a practical tool for assessing the effects of antipsychotic medication.

Consideration of the various perspectives has yielded research data that is useful in understanding, preventing, and treating the schizophrenic disorders. One way to combine the insights of the perspectives on the development and treatment of schizophrenic disorders is through the interactional model, which looks at the individual in interaction with the environment. Although this model can be applied to all behavior, in the area of schizophrenia it has been particularly clearly defined by Joseph Zubin (Zubin & Spring, 1977; Zubin, Magaziner, & Steinhauer, in press) in his vulnerability hypothesis.

This hypothesis assumes that schizophrenia is not a permanent disorder, but rather a permanent vulnerability to a disorder. Each person has a level of vulnerability to schizophrenia determined by genetic inheritance, prenatal and postnatal physical factors, and life experiences. Stressful life circumstances and events will then interact with the person's vulnerability. Zubin's theory assumes that if a person has no vulnerability to schizophrenia, no amount of stress will produce the disorder. If the combination exceeds a certain critical level, schizophrenic behavior will occur. When the stressors decrease the schizophrenic disorder will abate and the person will return to his or her earlier level of functioning.

Zubin believes that research, such as genetic studies and psychophysiological studies, can point out markers or characteristics that identify these vulnerable people. Efforts can then be directed to helping such individuals to avoid the degree of stress that might produce a schizophrenic disorder. This can be done both by providing a supportive environment and by helping vulnerable individuals to develop better coping skills so that the unavoidable stressors of life will not affect them so severely.

This view of schizophrenia has quite different implications from most of the perspectives I have discussed. It emphasizes the episodic nature of the disorder and pictures it as a set of behaviors that may come and go in a vulnerable individual depending on the stress in the environment. This is very unlike the view from the biological and psychodynamic perspectives, so that the presence of the disorder implies a generally poor prognosis for future functioning.

Data from Manfred Bleuler's long-term study of a group of individuals hospitalized for schizophrenia supports Zubin's idea that schizophrenia may be an episodic disorder (Bleuler, 1978). Bleuler found that about one third of the individuals had only one hospitalization from which they were released and were never rehospitalized. About 80 percent of the cases in both Bleuler's follow-up study and another long term follow-up (Ciompi, 1980) have either one or multiple hospitalizations followed by release.

Data from monozygotic twin studies consistently show that even individuals with identical heredity are not always concordant for schizophrenia. Zubin's idea of vulnerability is one way of understanding this fact. Most present day researchers, whether or not they agree with Zubin's statements, would agree no matter what their perspective that the development of a schizophrenic disorder is almost always a product of several factors including biological makeup, level of coping skills, environmental conditions, and life events.

One somewhat complex interaction model has been developed by Marzillier and Birchwood (1981). In this model they also make the assumption that there is an underlying vulnerability or deficit state (A). A schizophrenic episode (C) occurs only after acute psychosocial stress or life crisis (B). The episode leads to personal and social handicaps (D) that result from the schizophrenic episode. New episodes (B) are likely to occur if there are further psychosocial stresses or added psychosocial handicaps or negative aspects of treatment (B, D, and E). To prevent the disorder from becoming chronic, both social policy toward those who have been mentally ill and hospital treatment procedures need to be improved.

Anxiety Disorders

Whether or not we are living in the "Age of Anxiety," anxiety is a prevalent problem in contemporary life. Everyone has worries and fears. Freud argued that anxiety could be adaptive if the discomfort that goes along with it motivates people to learn new ways to approach life's challenges. But whether adaptive or maladaptive, the discomfort anxiety brings can be intense, with symptoms of motor tension, autonomic reactivity, apprehension about the future, and hypervigilance. The term *anxiety disorders* encompasses generalized reactions as well as more formalized conditions such as phobias, obsessions, and compulsions. While the disorientation and bizarreness of the neurotic pales in comparison to the more serious difficulties of the depressive or schizophrenic, the prevalence of the problem of anxiety is impressive. Surveys of the general population suggest that as many as one-third of all adults suffer from some nervous complaints, especially anxiety (Lader, 1975). This proportion is lower for males, the economically well-off, and the young, and higher for females, the elderly, and the poor.

Biological Approaches

In some cases these discoveries have led to specific medical methods of treatment. No direct organic cause has been found for most types of anxiety disorders, although in view of the findings of physical causation in other conditions, it becomes difficult to deny the possibility that they are somehow correlated with physical defects. For example, several studies have revealed some associations between anxiety and biophysical functioning. People whose nervous systems are particularly sensitive to stimulation seem more likely to experience severe anxiety. Inbreeding experiments with animals have shown that heredity strongly influences such characteristics as timidity, fearfulness, and aggressiveness. Evidence also shows that anxiety disorders tend to run in families. About 15 percent of parents and siblings of people with anxiety disorders are similarly affected (Carey & Gottesman,

1981). Monozygotic twins have more concordance (about 40 percent) for anxiety symptoms than do dizygotic twins (about 4 percent). While these findings suggest a genetic cause of anxiety, the results are not definitive because the subjects in this type of research not only have identical or similar heredities but usually also live together and thus experience similar environments.

Tranquilizing drugs are the most common somatic therapy used to relieve anxiety. While placebo and enthusiasm reactions may partly account for their effectiveness, some, such as the benzodiazepine tranquilizers (Valium, Librium), can be useful in reducing states of great tension. The literature on the behavioral effects of tranquilizer or antianxiety drugs suggests that these agents reduce the intensity of responses to stimuli that signal punishment and frustration. One problem with benzodiazepines is their side effects, which include drowsiness, lethargy, motor impairment, and reduced powers of concentration. The drugs also produce physiological and psychological dependence. Excessive use of these drugs may lead to undesirable behavior, including disorientation, confusion, rage, and other symptoms that resemble drunkenness.

Several years ago, researchers found that benzodiazepines bind to certain receptor sites and that the relative potencies of drugs in competing for these binding sites parallel their clinical effects. As pointed out earlier in the discussion of chemical transmission in affective disorders and in schizophrenia, these receptor sites serve as receiving stations for the brain's nerve cells and they are analogous to locks to which the appropriate chemicals fit as keys. The detailed localization of receptor sites has shed light on sites in the brain that mediate the effects of specific types of drugs. One animal study has shown that mice inbred for "emotionality" had fewer benzodiazepine receptors than "nonemotional" mouse strains (Robertson, 1979). Research on anxiety has also shown that some chemicals open these locks; others simply block the "keyhole" so that nothing else can get in, while still others seem to unlock different but related processes. Accordingly, a whole spectrum of drugs that influence anxiety level has been developed. One anxiety producer used in animal research is a chemical called betaCCE, which is a member of a family of substances known to have powerful effects on the nervous system.

Other drugs such as alcohol and barbiturates, which are sometimes used as calming agents by anxious individuals, do not bind to the benzodiazepine receptors. Future research will make clearer the mechanism by which antianxiety drugs exert their effects and may give rise to newer, more effective drugs that have fewer side-effects.

The discovery of receptor sites for antianxiety drugs has set off a widespread scientific search for other related details of the brain system. Some experts believe that receptor sites are a key to a natural anxiety system and that antianxiety drugs act in the same way as natural body substances, some of them perhaps still undiscovered, that keep anxiety in proper balance. One of the exciting possibilities now being investigated is that there may be substances produced within the body that attach to specific types of receptors.

Some drugs have specialized effects within the area of anxiety disorders. For example, imipramine, which is used in the treatment of depression, has made a contribution to the study of panic disorders. The indicators of panic reactions are similar to those seen in generalized anxiety disorders except that they are greatly magnified and have a sudden onset. People with panic disorders may not be anxious all the time. Instead they have unanticipated anxiety attacks that recur after periods (perhaps several days) of a return to normal functioning. Severe palpitations, extreme shortness of breath, chest pains or discomfort, trembling, sweating, dizziness, and feelings of helplessness mark the panic attacks, and the individual fears that he or she will die, go crazy, or do something uncontrolled. Panic attacks range in length from a few seconds to many hours and even days and vary in severity and in the degree of incapacitation involved.

Clinicians have often wondered whether panic attacks are simply very strong anxiety reactions. While imipramine has been shown to prevent the recurrence of panic attacks (Klein, 1981), it seems to have no effect on the anticipatory anxiety that panic attacks almost always arouse. Further biochemical research will probably provide additional pieces needed to solve the puzzle of panic attacks and how they fit into the category of anxiety disorders.

Psychological Approaches

Psychodynamic clinicians believe that the major determinants of anxiety disorders are intrapsychic events and unconscious motivations and that insight-oriented psychotherapy is the treatment of choice in helping people to overcome problems of anxiety. While many people report benefits from their psychotherapy experiences in psychodynamically oriented therapy, scientific demonstration of these benefits has been difficult to achieve (Salzman & Thaler, 1981). Beyond the question of how successfully psychotherapy relieves distress and improves behavioral functioning is the matter of what mechanisms are involved in psychotherapy when it is helpful.

The learning and cognitive points of view have resulted in a number of useful therapies for anxiety. For several anxiety disorders, particularly phobias, obsessions, and compulsions, exposure therapies seem to be the most effective clinical approach. Their basic characteristic is that the therapist strongly urges the client to encounter and to continue to attend to the anxiety-eliciting stimuli despite the initial stressful effects this usually entails. Two treatment procedures using exposure techniques are flooding and in vivo exposure. Flooding refers to therapist-controlled, prolonged imaginal exposure to high intensity fear-arousing stimulation. In vivo exposure is conducted in the presence of the actual fear-arousing stimulus and may be conducted with gradually increasing levels of stimulus intensity. A critical element of the treatment is motivating the client to maintain contact with noxious stimuli until he or she becomes used to them. This might mean, for example, exposing a compulsive handwasher to the evoking stimulus (dirt) while asking him or her to delay the handwashing response as long as possible. The therapist's task is to identify all components of the stimulus that evoke an avoidance or escape response and continue exposure until the need for the debilitating response no longer occurs.

Exposure treatment of phobias and obsessive-compulsive disorders has produced consistently good results with lasting improvements for up to several years (Barlow & Wolfe, 1981; Marks, 1981). The longer the exposure to the critical stimulus, the better the results. Individuals who, on their own, mentally rehearse being exposed to the upsetting, fear-arousing situation show high levels of improvement (Biran & Wilson, 1981). The commonest reason for failure to improve is noncompliance with treatment instructions, particularly concerning the need for clients to seek exposure to fear-arousing stimuli when outside the therapeutic session. An important task for future research is finding out why exposure is effective. When a client "gets used to" an upsetting stimulus, what is going on? One possible explanation for the effectiveness of exposure treatment is that as clients observe their ability to maintain even a little exposure to upsetting stimuli, they gain confidence in themselves and develop a new cognitive set that encourages them to persist in their efforts to overcome their problems.

Psychosocial Processes and Physical Symptoms

Each person can be regarded as a living system made up of interacting biological, psychological, and social subsystems. Biological subsystems that influence health and illness have been studied over a period of many years. Psychological and social subsystems that contribute to physical illness have only recently received intensive study. There are indications that these subsystems may be of considerable importance.

Personality and Health

Although more evidence is needed, temperament and personality assessed early in life may be predictive of susceptibility to illness decades later. In one study that demonstrated this, Rorschach tests were given routinely over a number of years to Johns Hopkins University medical students (Graves & Thomas, 1981). At the time of testing the students were in good health. The researchers developed special ways of rating Rorschach responses in which figures in the inkblots were described as interacting in some way with each other (for example, "Two small children arguing," "Two bears fighting"). The interaction ratings ranged from warm, affectionate, and close (for example, "People kissing") to violent and destructive (for example, "A witch committing a murder"). Twenty to twenty-five years later, the health status of each subject was assessed. Those whose Rorschachs reflected either a relatively restricted capacity for emotional relationships with or ambivalence about their ties to others were especially prone to develop cancer in later life. The future cancer victims showed a relative lack of well-balanced patterns of social relationships. Especially interesting was the finding that the Rorschachs of subjects who at midlife were either healthy or had cardiovascular disorders, tended to be similar to each other, but different from the Rorschachs of subjects who developed either cancer or a mental disorder. The Rorschachs of these latter two groups tended to be similar. These results suggest the value of exploring the linkages of emotional and social orientations with physiological and biological systems.

Although at the present time all we have are clues concerning the role of psychosocial factors in cancer, there already exists a sizable body of research indicating that psychological and social factors play important roles in cardiovascular disorders. For example, there is growing evidence that people who show a Type A behavior pattern are more prone to have heart attacks. People who show a Type A pattern tend to

- Talk rapidly and at times explosively
- Move, walk, and eat rapidly
- Become unduly irritated at delay (for example, waiting in line)
- Attempt to schedule more and more in less and less time
- Feel vaguely guilty while relaxing
- Try to do two things at once.

Type A tendencies have been assessed using both interview and questionnaire formats. Regardless of how assessed, Type A individuals are competitive, continually strive for achievement, and are aggressive in their orientation toward life. Their families and associates describe them as hyperalert, restless, and impatient. Type A tendencies have been assessed reliably in young, low-risk age groups as well as among the middle-aged. Type A college students show more involvement in extra-curricular activities, better academic performance, and higher aspirations for academic success than do Type Bs (Ovcharchyn, Johnson, & Petzel, 1981).

One source of information on Type A behavior is the Framingham, Massachusetts, study, a longitudinal investigation concerning factors in heart disease that was begun in 1948. One subgroup of 1,674 Framingham participants between 45 and 77 years of age were assessed for Type A tendencies and then followed up over an eight-year period. The Type A investigation began when they responded to a questionnaire whose items dealt with aggressiveness, ambitiousness, competitive drive, and a longstanding sense of time urgency (Haynes, Feinleich, & Kannel, 1980). There was a significant association of Type A behavior with coronary heart disease among white-collar and blue-collar men in the 45–64 and 65–74 year age groups, the association being stronger among men holding white-collar jobs. Women between the ages of 45 and 64 years who developed coronary heart disease also scored significantly higher on the Framingham Type A measure and showed more tension, anxiety, and related tendencies than women who remained free of coronary heart disease. The Type A women developed twice as much coronary heart disease as Type B women. While working women tended to have higher Type A scores than housewives, being a housewife did not protect Type A women from higher rates of coronary disease. Working women under 65 years of age were almost twice as likely to develop coronary disease if they exhibited the Type A rather than Type B behavior. Among housewives in these same groups, coronary heart disease incidence in Type As was almost three times greater than among Type Bs.

In general, the results of the Framingham study suggest that the Type A behavior pattern operates independently of the usual coronary risk factors (such as blood pressure, age, and weight). There is evidence that the Type A behavior pattern, especially in combination with suppressed anger, is an important risk factor for coronary heart disease in both men and women.

A long-range goal of research on the Type A pattern is the development of educational and therapeutic programs that can modify the maladaptive behavior—such as preoccupation with time pressure—that results in coronary heart disease. Group therapy, conducted along cognitive and behavioral lines, may be effective in modifying Type A tendencies. In one study, groups of Type A individuals were taught how to alter a variety of behaviors including certain speech patterns (e.g., interrupting), psychomotor actions (e.g., emphatic gesturing), and other physical activities (e.g., hurried walking) (Thoresen, Telch, & Eagleston, 1981). In addition, the subjects learned relaxation skills and were encouraged to evaluate many of their basic beliefs. While only long-term follow-up can show whether or not the group therapy reduces coronary heart disease risks, there is some evidence that it does weaken Type A behavior tendencies.

Communication, Recovery, and Health Behavior

Psychologists are playing an increasingly useful role in enhancing communication in medical settings. This is illustrated by a variety of research endeavors. Two examples discussed here are projects in which presurgical patients are prepared for what is going to happen to them and efforts to strengthen pro-health behavior in the general population through the use of the mass media. Research shows that patients who find out about the medical treatment they will be getting beforehand develop more effective ways of coping with the stress of illness than patients who do not obtain such information. Four kinds of information play important roles in the response of patients to illness and treatment.

1. Information about the nature of the illness and the medical reasons for initiating particular treatments
2. Information describing the medical procedures to be carried out step-by-step
3. Information about particular sensations (for example, pain or the possible side effects of medication)
4. Information about coping strategies that can be used in adjusting to the upcoming threat.

Whether or not patients use the information available to them and whether or not they follow medical advice depends on several factors other than the information given and how it is presented. For instance, those who do not see themselves as in control of their lives may not carry out the steps needed to regain health, such as following instructions about exercise and medication. Less educated patients are more likely than those who are better educated to break medical appointments and not to follow medical advice. Patients who express their concerns to their doctors and receive answers in simple language tend to experience less stress about their physical conditions. Researchers in the area of behavioral medicine are carrying out extensive investigations of the types of information that are medically useful and the best ways of communicating the information. Free communication between patients and health-care providers has been shown to be especially important. Without it, patients' fears stay bottled up and their misconceptions cannot be corrected. Self-help groups, made up of patients with a similar diagnosis, can provide needed social support as well as encourage the communication of information.

Audiovisual techniques have been used to aid in recovery from illness and to stimulate the promotion of healthful behavior. The use of films and videotapes in conveying information to patients is illustrated by Melamed's (1979) research with children undergoing painful dental procedures. She showed the children films of other children as they proceeded through the treatment and found that those who saw the informative film exhibited less disruptive behavior, reported less apprehension, and showed better clinical progress than did children in control comparison goups. In other words, their coping abilities had increased. This sort of preparatory procedure is particularly effective with people who experience high levels of worry, emotional tension, and anxiety before and during medical procedures (Shipley, Butt, & Horwitz, 1979).

Psychologists are also actively investigating use of the media to promote healthful behavior. Films, videotapes, and pamphlets have been used effectively in several limited focus community education programs to provide information about such health hazards as smoking and obesity. An ambitious study aimed at preventing heart disease by changing health-related behaviors is being carried on at Stanford University by a team of psychologists and physicians. In this study, carried out in three communities, they are using television and radio programs, direct mail, newspaper columns and ads, billboards, bus posters, and recorded telephone messages. This mass media information includes facts about the effects of smoking and obesity, an explanation of how the heart functions, diet tips (including how to prepare simple, healthful meals), and ideas about how individuals can get more exercise. The evidence gathered indicates that this heart disease prevention program is working. Reductions in smoking and better health habits have been noted among the subjects. The best results were found among those who had exposure to the mass media campaign but also participated in special classes (Maccoby & Alexander 1980; Nash & Farquhar, 1980).

Health psychologists are especially interested in identifying and strengthening life styles that contribute to well-being. The need for improvement in healthful life styles is shown by a few statistics. It has been estimated that 40 to 80 million people in the United States are overweight and eat nutritionally inadequate diets. About 50 million individuals in this country are smokers, and approximately 9 million abuse alcohol. Smoking and drinking are self-destructive behavior with profound personal, social, and economic implications. Much self-destructive behavior is not accompanied by unpleasant symptoms in the early stages and unfortunately the medical consequences may go unnoticed until the damage has already occurred.

DSM III

Having reviewed the contributions of theories of maladaptation to the advancement of knowledge about abnormal behavior, it is perhaps ironically fitting to end this article on a somewhat atheoretical note although one highly pertinent to the study of abnormal psychology.

The third edition of the American Psychiatric Association's Diagnostic and Statistical Manual (DSM III) was introduced in 1980, amid fanfare and controversy. It is now the primary basis for clinical communication and classifying psychological and behavioral problems. For that reason alone, independent of whether it is an improvement over other diagnostic approaches, knowledge of it is important.

DSM III differs from earlier classification manuals in its emphasis on describing, rather than interpreting, clinical problems. This change in focus came about because of concern that unreliability of psychiatric diagnosis often arises from too high a degree of guesswork about the underlying causes of problems. The clinicians and researchers who developed DSM III (1) introduced more precise language into the classification system, (2) increased the coverage of the manual to classify additional types of maladaptive behavior, and (3) provided more examples of the various categories. As a consequence, DSM III is about ten times longer than DSM II, which was published in 1960. The greater complexity of DSM III reflects not only the need for a more reliable classification system but also the growth in knowledge about maladaptive behavior.

DSM III uses what is called a multiaxial classification system. This means that instead of simply placing an individual in one category (for example, schizophrenia) each case is characterized in terms of a number of clinically important factors. There are five axes in DSM III; the use of the last two are recommended but not required.

Axis 1 contains the primary classification or diagnosis of the problem that requires attention (for example, fear of heights).

Axis 2 describes ingrained, inflexible aspects of personality (such as the tendency to be overly suspicious of the motives of others) that may influence the client's behavior and treatability.

Axis 3 refers to any physical disorders that seem relevant to a case (for example, the client's history of heart attacks).

Axis 4 rates the severity of psychosocial stressors in the recent past that may have contributed to the clinical problem and that might influence the course of treatment (for example, divorce, death of a parent, loss of job).

Axis 5 contains an estimate of the highest level of adaptive functioning attained by the client in the areas of social relationships, occupational activities, and the use of leisure time.

One of the major objectives of DSM III was to be quite specific about the criteria for using the various diagnostic categories. It seems generally to have been successful in achieving this objective. It also seems to have been successful in reducing the amount of inference needed to make a particular diagnosis by emphasizing description of behavior rather than ideas about cause. The basis for this objective is that the more inference needed to form a judgment, the greater the likelihood of disagreement concerning the judgment. In working towards these objectives, DSM III has taken a primarily descriptive, rather than theoretical approach to abnormal behavior.

The multiaxial approach is a step forward because it recognizes that classification involves several different elements that are not alternatives to one another. By introducing axes that pertain to severity of stress and previous level of adjustment, as well as to long-lasting personality patterns, recognition is given to the need for integrating what is known about the person's vulnerabilities, assets, and stressful life events. In addition to increasing the dimensions used in describing particular disorders, DSM III has also greatly increased its coverage of the range of disorders. This increase is especially evident in the way it deals with disorders of childhood. DSM III recognizes that although some childhood disorders may persist into adult life, others seem to be outgrown.

Although many classification specialists welcome DSM III's comprehensive approach, not all would agree that its diagnostic categories are the right ones, that is, that the categories are meaningful and important. To what extent should children's reading and arithmetic difficulties be regarded, as DSM III does, as clinical problems? Inclusion of these developmental problems in a psychiatric classification system seems, at least, questionable.

It is possible that the DSM III's comprehensiveness will prove to be a mixed blessing. Research on agreement among clinicians in classifying patients has shown that there is a high level of agreement on broad general diagnostic categories, such as depression and juvenile delinquency, and low reliability for finer subdivisions within these general categories (Rutter & Shaffer, 1980). Much research will be needed to determine the breadth and specificity needed to maximize the value of DSM III and other systems used in classifying abnormal behavior (Frances & Cooper, 1981).

Despite the justifiable criticisms that can be made of DSM III, there seems little doubt that it is an improvement over previous diagnostic systems. Many of DSM III's limitations grow out of limitations in our understanding of what mental health and mental disorder are. For example, even experts who have devoted their entire careers to studying schizophrenia may not agree on the boundaries of the concept of schizophrenia. No classification system can be any better than current attitudes and knowledge concerning the subject of the classification, be it people, plants, or rock formations.

Conclusion

The goal of this paper has been to provide a brief overview of some of the most active areas within psychology that relate to the study of abnormal behavior. The first of these is the increasing similarity of formerly rather disparate theoretical viewpoints. This does not suggest that theorists of all persuasions are in agreement—that is far from the case. However, it does mean that important aspects of one view have been incorporated into others. For example, psychodynamic theorists have always been interested in the history of the individual, but the history they concentrated on was a history of events. Recently at least some psychodynamic theorists have begun to focus on the history of cognitions as well. Learning theorists have also become more interested in cognitions. Their focus on behavior has broadened to include this new category. Seligman's helplessness theory of depression is an example of a learning theory that was expanded and modified to include cognitive elements, in this case causal attributions, as an important factor. Most learning-based therapies now include a great deal of emphasis on the learning of new and adaptive cognitions. The work of Lewinsohn is an example. Cognitive theory also is changing. For example, the cognitive therapeutic approach of Beck and his co-workers has broadened to include behavior checklists and homework assignments of the type typically used by learning-oriented therapists. Cognitive therapists also have begun to look at the history of the client's cognitions. Some biologically oriented research efforts, particularly those related to a variety of physical illnesses, are becoming more sophisticated about the need to include psychological factors such as cognitions and personality factors as independent variables.

Because in the last few years the biological and cognitive perspectives have shown the most change and have served as the focus of an increasing amount of research, these two areas have been emphasized in this review. The rapidly growing role of psychology in health-related areas also has been especially noted. Finally, this review has briefly touched on the characteristics of the revised classification system, the DSM III, now in use by care-giving professionals and researchers. Some of the new criteria for diagnosing disorders such as schizophrenia and the affective disorders are already beginning to affect research findings, because the groups studied under these new criteria have somewhat different characteristics than groups earlier identified by the same or similar terms.

Perhaps the most important goal of this review is to illustrate how the use of contrasting theoretical frameworks can enhance the teaching of abnormal psychology, first, by aiding the student to organize the material in a meaningful way and, second, by fostering new insights into the significance of the behavior observed.

Reference Note

Beck, A. T., Rush, J. A., Shaw, B. R., & Emery, G. *Cognitive therapy of depression: A treatment manual.* Unpublished manuscript, 1978.

References

Abramson, L., Seligman, M. E. P., & Teasdale, J. D. Learned helplessness in humans: Critique and reformulation. *Journal of Abnormal Psychology*, 1978, *87*, 49–74.

Akiskal, H. S. Concepts of depression. In E. Friedman, J. Mann, & S. Gershon (Eds.), *Depression and antidepressants: Implications for cause and treatment*. New York: Raven Press, 1981.

American Psychiatric Association. *Diagnositc and statistical manual of mental disorders* (3rd ed.). Washington, DC: Author, 1980.

Barlow, D. H., & Wolfe, B. E. Behavioral approaches to anxiety disorders: A report on the NIMH-SUNY, Albany, research conference. *Journal of Consulting and Clinical Psychology*, 1981, *49*, 448–454.

Beck, A. T. *Depression: Clinical, experimental, and theoretical aspects*. New York: Hoeber, 1967.

Bieber, I. *Cognitive Psychoanalysis*. New York: Jason Aronson, 1980.

Biran, M., & Wilson, G. T. Treatment of phobic disorders using cognitive and exposure: A self-efficacy analysis. *Journal of Consulting and Clinical Psychology*, 1981, *49*, 886–889.

Blatt, S. J., D'Afflitti, J. P., & Quinlan, D. M. Experiences of depression in normal young adults. *Journal of Abnormal Psychology*, 1976, *85*, 383–389.

Bleuler, M. *The schizophrenic disorders: Long-term patient and family studies*. New Haven: Yale University Press, 1978.

Bowers, M. B., Jr. Biochemical processes in schizophrenia: An update. *Special report: Schizophrenia 1980*. Rockville, MD: U.S. Department of Health and Human Services, 1981, 27–37.

Bowlby, J. *Loss: Sadness and depression*. New York: Basic Books, 1980.

Brown, G. W., Harris, T., & Copeland, J. R. Depression and loss. *British Journal of Psychiatry*, 1977, *130*, 1–18.

Carey, G., & Gottesman, I. I. Twin and family studies of anxiety, phobic and obsessive disorders. In D. F. Klein & J. Rabkin (Eds.), *Anxiety: New Research and Changing Concepts*. New York: Raven Press, 1981.

Cowen, E. L. Help is where you find it: Four informal helping groups. *American Psychologist*, 1982, *37*, 385–395.

Carroll, G. J., Feinberg, M., Greden, J., Tarika, J., Albala, A. A., Haskett, R. F., James, N., Kronfol, Z., Lohr, N., Steiner, M., deVigne, J. P., & Young, E. A specific laboratory test for the diagnosis of melancholia. *Archives of General Psychiatry*, 1981, *38*, 15–27.

Ciompi, L. The natural history of schizophrenia in the long term. *British Journal of Psychiatry*, 1980, *136*, 413–420.

Crook, T., & Eliot, J. Parental death during childhood and adult depression: A critical review of the literature. *Psychological Bulletin*, 1980, *87*, 252–259.

Derry, P. A., & Kuiper, N. A. Schematic processing and self reference in clinical depression. *Journal of Abnormal Psychology*, 1981, *90*, 286–297.

Doane, J. A., West, K. L., Goldstein, M. J., Rodnick, E. H., & Jones, J. E. Parental affective style and communication deviance as predictors of subsequent schizophrenia spectrum disorders in vulnerable adolescents. *Archives of General Psychiatry*, 1981, *38*, 679–685.

Dollard, J., & Miller, N. *Personality and psychotherapy*. New York: McGraw-Hill, 1950.

Frances, A., & Cooper, A. M. Descriptive and dynamic psychiatry: A perspective on DSM III. *American Journal of Psychiatry*, 1981, *138*, 1198–1202.

Freud, S. Mourning and melancholia. In J. Strachey (Ed.), *The standard edition of the complete psychological works of Sigmund Freud* (Vol. 14). London: Hogarth Press, 1957 (Originally published, 1917.)

Graves, P. L., & Thomas, C. B. Themes of interaction in medical student's Rorschach responses as predictors of midlife health or disease. *Psychosomatic Medicine*, 1981, *43*, 215–225.

Harlow, H. F., & Suomi, S. J. Induced depression in monkeys. *Behavioral Biology*, 1974, *12*, 273–296.

Hammen, D., & deMayo, R. Cognitive correlates of teacher stress and depressive symptoms: Implications for attributional models of depression. *Journal of Abnormal Psychology*, 1982, *91*, 96–101.

Haynes, S. G., Feinleich, M., & Kannel, W. B. The relationship of psychological factors to coronary heart disease in the Framingham study: III. Eight year incidence of coronary heart disease. *American Journal of Epidemiology*, 1980, *111*, 37–58.

Johnson, M. H., & Holzman, P. S. *The measurement of thought disorder*. San Francisco: Jossey-Bass, 1979.

Kessler, S. The genetics of schizophrenia: A review. *Special report: Schizophrenia, 1980*. Rockville, MD: U.S. Department of Health and Human Services, 1981.

Klein, D. F. Anxiety reconceptualized. In D. F. Klein & J. G. Rabkin (Eds.), *Anxiety: New research and changing concepts*. New York: Raven Press, 1981.

Kupfer, D. J., Foster, G. F., Coble, P., McPartland, R. J., & Ulrich, F. The application of EEG sleep for the differential diagnosis of affective disorders. *American Journal of Psychiatry*, 1978, *135*, 69–74.

Lader, M. The nature of clinical anxiety in modern society. In C. D. Speilberger & I. G. Sarason (Eds.), *Stress and anxiety* (Vol. 1). Washington, DC: Hemisphere, 1975.

Lewinsohn, P. M., & Arconad, M. Behavioral treatment in depression: A social learning approach. In J. Clarkin & H. Glazer (Eds.), *Behavioral and directive treatment strategies*. New York: Garland Publishing, 1981.

Lewinsohn, P. M., Lobitz, W. C., & Wilson, S. "Sensitivity" of depressed individuals to aversive stimuli. *Journal of Abnormal Psychology*, 1973, *79*, 291–295.

Lewinsohn, P. M., Mischel, W., Chaplin, W., & Barton, R. Social competence and depression: The role of illusory self-perceptions. *Journal of Abnormal Psychology*, 1980, *89*, 203–212.

Lewinsohn, P. M., & Talkington, J. Studies on the measurement of unpleasant events and relations with depression. *Applied Psychological Measurement*, 1979, *3*, 83–101.

Maccoby N., & Alexander, J. Use of media in lifestyle programs. In P. O. Davidson & S. M. Davidson (Eds.), *Behavioral medicine: Changing health lifestyles*. New York: Brunner/Mazel, 1980.

Marks, I. M. Review of behavioral psychotherapy: I. Obsessive-compulsive disorders. *American Journal of Psychiatry*, 1981, *138*, 584–592.

Marzillier, J. S., & Birchwood, M. J. Behavioral treatment of cognitive disorders. In L. Michelson, M. Hersen, & S. M. Turner (Eds.), *Future perspectives on behavior therapy*. New York: Plenum Press, 1981.

Melamed, B. G. Behavior approaches to fear in dental settings. In M. Herson, R. M. Eisler, & P. M. Miller (Eds.), *Progress in behavior modification* (Vol. 7). New York: Academic Press, 1979.

Miller, I. W., & Norman, W. H. Learned helplessness in humans: A review and attribution-theory model. *Psychological Bulletin*, 1979, *86*, 93–118.

Nash, J. D., & Farquhar, J. W. Applications of behavioral medicine to disease prevention in a total community setting: A review of the three-community study. In J. M. Ferguson & C. B. Taylor (Eds.), *The comprehensive handbook of behavioral medicine.* New York: Spectrum Publishing, 1980.

National Center for Health Statistics. *The nation's use of health resources, 1980* (DHEW Publication No. PHS 80–1240). Hyattsville, MD: Author, 1980.

Nielsen, A. C. III, & Williams, T. A. Depression in ambulatory medical patients: Prevalence by self report questionnaire and recognition by non-psychiatric physicians. *Archives of General Psychiatry,* 1980, *37,* 999–1002.

Ovcharchyn, C. A., Johnson, H. H., & Petzel, T. P. Type A behavior, academic aspirations, and academic success. *Journal of Personality,* 1981, *49,* 247–256.

Pilisuk, M. Delivery of social support: The serial inoculation. *American Journal of Orthopsychiatry,* 1982, *52,* 20–31.

Robertson, H. A. Benzodiazepine receptors in "emotional" and "nonemotional" mice: Comparison of four strains. *European Journal of Pharmacology,* 1979, *56,* 163.

Rutter, M., & Shaffer, D. DSM III: A step forward or back in terms of the classification of child psychiatric disorders. *Journal of the American Academy of Child Psychiatry,* 1980, *19,* 371–394.

Salzman, L., & Thaler, F. H. Obsessive-compulsive disorders: A review of the literature. *American Journal of Psychiatry,* 1981, *138,* 286–296.

Sarason, I. G. Three lacunae of cognitive therapy. *Cognitive Therapy and Research.* 1979, *3,* 223–235.

Schildkraut, J. J. The colecholamine hypothesis of affective disorders: A review of supporting evidence. *American Journal of Psychiatry,* 1965, *122,* 509–522.

Scovern, A. W., & Kilman, P. R. Status of electroconvulsive therapy: Review of the outcome literature. *Psychological Bulletin,* 1980, *87,* 260–303.

Seligman, M. E. P. Depression and learned helplessness. In R. J. Friedman & M. M. Katz (Eds.), *The psychology of depression: Contemporary theory and research.* Washington, DC: V. H. Winston, 1974.

Seligman, M. E. P. *Helplessness: On depression, development, and death.* San Francisco: Freeman, 1975.

Shipley, R. H., Butt, J. H., & Horowitz, E. A. Preparations to reexperience a stressful medical examination: Effect of repetitious videotape exposure and coping style. *Journal of Consulting and Clinical Psychology,* 1979, *47,* 485–492.

Sulser, F. Pharmacology: New cellular mechanisms of antidepressant drugs. In S. Fielding & R. C. Effland (Eds.), *New Frontiers in Psychotropic Drug Research.* Mount Kisco, NY: Futura, 1979.

Thoreson, C. E., Telch, M. J., & Eagleston, J. R. Approaches to altering the Type A behavior pattern. *Psychosomatics,* 1981, *22,* 472–482.

Vogel, G. W., Vogel, F., McAbee, R. S., & Thurmond, A. J. Improvement of depression by REM sleep deprivation. *Archives of General Psychiatry,* 1980, *37,* 247–253.

Wyatt, R. J., Potkin, S. G., & Murphy, D. L. Platelet MAO activity in schizophrenia: A review of the data. *American Journal of Psychiatry,* 1979, *136,* 377–385.

Wynne, L. C., Singer, M. T., Bartko, J. J., & Toohey, M. L. Schizophrenics and their families: Research on parental communication. In J. M. Tanner (Ed.), *Developments in psychiatric research.* London: Hodder & Stoughton, 1977.

Zubin, J., Magaziner, J., & Steinhauer, S. R. *The metamorphosis of schizophrenia: From chronicity to vulnerability.* Unpublished paper, University of Pittsburgh Medical School, 1982.

COMMENTS

The abnormal psychology unit of the introductory psychology course raises unique issues. Many students have preconceived ideas regarding pyschopathology. Some of its vocabulary has become a part of conversational English, having acquired a popular meaning quite different from the professional one. Such misconceptions may require correction before students can learn new materials.

Sarason observes that he had neither taught nor demonstrated ability to teach prior to obtaining his first (and current) employment. Since lack of teaching experience is common among newly graduated psychologists, presentations from "veterans" like Sarason serve an even more important function than may be apparent at first glance. The beginning instructor devotes years to "learning how to teach" and developing specialized, independent research programs. Meanwhile, progress in other subspecialties of psychology continues, and lecture materials for the introductory psychology course may become outdated without the instructor's really being aware of these changes. So, although the instructor's presentation may have improved, the purpose of the delivery is no longer adequately served.

Another issue that may arise when teaching psychopathology is the integration of theory and application. Traditionally, several lectures are devoted to the major theoretical perspectives and then are followed by a presentation on the major diagnostic categories. This can leave students with the impression that there is no confluence among theories and a minimal relationship between theory and application. Sarason has dealt with this problem by presenting one of the better described diagnostic categories, depression, from different perspectives. (The instructor could select the diagnostic category with which he or she feels most comfortable.) The importance of research as well as the latest findings are easily included within one lecture using this approach.

Teaching psychopathology can illustrate interrelations among subfields of psychology. A knowledge of physiological psychology is important in comprehending pharmacological treatments. The relationship of learning theory to behavior therapy is another example. Integration helps the student appreciate the discipline as a whole rather than as a collection of fragmented subspecialties.

Teaching abnormal psychology provides numerous opportunities to draw on events from daily living. The morning news can be integrated with lecture materials: The Type A personality is a good example. Quizzes designed to assess this characteristic have appeared in popular publications. References to stress can lead into a discussion of stereotypes of people in certain occupations. The instructor can then easily integrate findings from research on such people as astronauts and fighter pilots. The research cited by Sarason on the impact of parental interaction during early years on later personality development within the context of certain professions invites discussion of the interaction of developmental and abnormal psychology.

A common issue faced by academicians is the extent to which special presentations contribute to effective teaching. Sarason suggests alternatives to the lecture that can be tailored by the instructor to each class. A role-play situation illustrating abnormal behavior may be more effective than the available films on the topic. The instructor could pose as a psychiatric patient who is interviewed in front of the class. The instructor will need a confederate trained to interview. It may be possible for several faculty members to develop a role-play to be used in each other's classes. The role-play can then be used from year to year with only slight modifications. If graduate students are available, they may prove good interviewers. The simulated interview can be followed by discussion of the questions asked as well as the behaviors illustrated. Sarason suggests audiotaping the presentation so that students can listen to the tape in the university's media center. Many students who attended live interviews chose to listen again.

Sarason also noted that he now uses fewer films than in the beginning of his academic career. Besides becoming more comfortable with the act of teaching, the more experienced instructor has developed a more critical eye about films. The beginning instructor can consult with mentors to find a few good films within the instructor's budget.

Guest lecturers are useful to the introductory psychology professor whose specialty within the discipline is in some other area. A practicing clinician could talk about the changes that have occurred in the profession during his or her career. One or two guest lecturers a semester provide enough variety without giving the students the impression that their professor has either too little knowledge or too little interest in teaching. The level of sophistication of the students should be explained to the prospective speaker.

Sarason's suggestion that students read a first-person account of psychopathology may be more applicable to the first course in abnormal psychology than it is to the introductory psychology course. An extra credit project, however, most apropos for the section on abnormal psychology, would be a written report on one of several first-person accounts of psychopathology.

Any academician could profit from Sarason's discussion of recent developments in abnormal psychology. The methods he suggests are adaptable to the skills, interests, and situation of the individual instructor.

K. E. MOYER

THE PHYSIOLOGY
OF MOTIVATION:
AGGRESSION
AS A MODEL

K. E. Moyer joined the faculty of Carnegie-Mellon University after receiving his doctorate from Washington University in St. Louis. In 1954 Moyer served as a consultant on higher education to the government of Norway. He is a fellow of the Division of Psychopharmacology, American Psychological Association, and a fellow of the American Association for the Advancement of Science. He was the first editor-in-chief of the international journal *Aggressive Behavior* from 1975 to 1978. Moyer has published over 100 items including seven books, nineteen chapters in books by other authors, and articles in four encyclopedias. In 1954 he was awarded the Carnegie Foundation Award for Excellence in Teaching.

K. E. MOYER

THE PHYSIOLOGY OF MOTIVATION: AGGRESSION AS A MODEL

A s professors, we have a strange profession indeed. Society assigns to us an important role, the training of the young, but makes no provision for teaching us how to teach. Like many professors, I never had the opportunity to take a course on how to lecture or how to lead a class discussion. Perhaps even more important, I was given no insight into how to counsel young people who, having just failed my course, were having anxiety over facing their parents.

It might be suggested that teachers should be experts on teaching because they have suffered under so much for so long. I am reminded, however, that clinicians say that the abused child frequently becomes the abusive adult.

Although I can claim no expertise, I would like to discuss some factors involved in the lecture process. I will then give a lecture.

The lecture is probably the most used and the most abused of the teaching techniques. It has, however, a dubious pedagogical base. Obviously, if it can be spoken, it can be written down, and if it can be written down, it can be xeroxed and given to students, who can then read the lecture in half the time it takes to listen to it.

Overall, the lecture is a very poor method for transmitting information. Books, if they are read, are much better. The lecture does

This paper is based in part on, and is an extension of, the author's earlier works. A more detailed presentation of some of the concepts may be found in Moyer's *The Psychobiology of Aggression* (1976).

have value, however, beyond its content. Obscure points in the text can be cleared up during the lecture. The lecture gives moderate assurance that students have been exposed to a particular portion of the course material. The lecture can motivate and, at its best, can inspire. For reasons that are not immediately clear, it is easier for many people to come to a lecture rather than to read it.

Humor can and should be used. It is considerable help to the weary student who comes to class after a late night or all-night study session. It has been said that if you don't get three laughs an hour, you are a boring lecturer and your students are asleep. I am not so sure about that, but I believe that "Funny is not enough." Humor, for the greatest impact, must be relevant. If it is not, it distracts. If it is, it reinforces the point being made.

Slides are a useful adjunct to some lectures. Someone has said that an expert can be defined as an individual 25 miles from home with a box of slides. The value of slides is obvious, but it should be pointed out that they can be more distracting than edifying. The first distraction occurs when no one knows where the light switch is. The second occurs when the operator does not know how to work the projector. Finally, because of the innate perversity of inanimate objects, the slides are all upside down.

In the course of a lecture, one can always determine how he or she is doing and adjust the lecture accordingly. In each audience there are responders. These are the people who listen intently and nod their heads and smile when a good point is made and frown slightly when a point is obscure. When these individuals stare straight ahead and their eyes glaze over, it means trouble.

As an audience of psychology instructors, my readers have at least one thing in common. You all have an extensive knowledge of motivation. As I develop a model of aggressive behavior, I would like to have you consider whether that model is useful in integrating the large amount of material that comes under the heading of motivation.

Aggression and Motivation

It should be pointed out first that aggression, like motivation, is not a unitary construct. There are a number of different kinds of motivation and of aggressive behavior (Brain, 1979; Moyer, 1968). This means that it is not going to be possible to construct a single model that will fit all of them in detail. However, I can deal with the mechanisms or kinds of mechanisms that are common to many of the different kinds of aggressive behavior.

The basic premise of this aggression/motivation model is that the brains of animals and humans have neural systems that, when fired in the presence of a relevant target, result in aggressive or destructive behavior toward that target. In the case of humans, aggressive behavior may be controlled, but the individual will still have the appropriate feelings of hostility. There is now abundant evidence to support that premise.

Some of the most fundamental work in this area was done by John Flynn at Yale (Egger & Flynn, 1963). He has worked with cats and has enlarged on techniques that were developed in the early 1940s. It is possible to implant an electrode in specific areas deep in an animal's brain. The electrode can be attached to a plug that is cemented to the skull. The plug can then be attached to a stimulation source making it possible to stimulate the brain of an animal that is awake and free to move around. When the experiment is finished for the day, the subject can be returned to its home cage none the worse for the experience.

The cats used by Flynn were nonpredatory and would not normally attack rats. Some, in fact, would live with a rat for months and not molest it. Flynn and one of his graduate students discovered that if an electrode implanted in the cat's lateral hypothalamus is electrically activated, the animal will ignore the experimenter standing there, but it will immediately attack and kill an available rat. The kill will be quite precise, resulting from a bite in the cervical region of the spinal cord in the typical predatory behavior of the feline. However, if the electrode is located in the medial portion of the lateral hypothalamus, and the cat is stimulated in the presence of the rat, it will ignore the rat, and turn and attack the experimenter. The attack on the experimenter will be highly directed; it is not similar to the random attacks of a decerebrate animal. This cat apparently intends to do the experimenter harm, and in fact, it will. For additional studies, see Bandler (1979); Bandler and Fatouris (1978); and Bandler, Halliday, and Abeyewardene (1980). Also see Kruk and Van der Poel (1980, pp. 385–390), Kruk, Van der Poel, and de Vos-Frerichs (1979), and Fuchs, Dalsass, Siegel, and Siegel (1981).

One particularly interesting experiment was done by Robinson and his colleagues (Robinson, Alexander, & Bowne, 1969). They took a small Rhesus monkey and implanted an electrode in the anterior hypothalamus. They put the animal in a primate chair, activated the electrode, and showed that the monkey did not become aggressive towards inanimate objects, nor did it become aggressive towards the experimenter. It was then put in a cage with two other monkeys; one that was larger and dominant to the experimental animal, and the other the dominant monkey's female consort. When stimulated the experimental monkey vigorously and immediately attacked only the dominant male monkey. It did not attack the female. This appeared to be a valid primate attack because the dominant monkey reacted by counterattacking just as viciously as it usually would have if attacked by a submissive animal. After this scenario was repeated a number of times, Robinson et al. found that the dominance relationship changed: The stimulation-induced attacks were so intense that the formerly dominant animal ultimately became submissive to the experimental monkey.

This experiment shows first that the particular brain stimulation used resulted in one specific kind of aggression, which I have called "inter-male," that is, the specific tendency for one male to attack another. Second, this experiment demonstrates that aggressive behavior is stimulus bound. In the absence of the relevant stimulus, that monkey, even though stimulated time and again, showed no irritability or increased tendency to attack other targets.

It is important not to generalize too quickly from one species to another. One must be particularly cautious in generalizing from animals to man. However, we now have good evidence that human beings, despite encephalization, have not escaped from the neural determinants of their aggressive behavior. There are now several hundred people who have electrodes implanted in their brains. The wires are attached to small sockets cemented to the skull. These patients can be brought into the laboratory, plugged in, and precise areas deep in the brain can be electrically stimulated (Heath, 1981, pp. 176–194).

A case reported by King (1961, pp. 477–486) is particularly instructive. The patient in this experiment was a mild-mannered woman who was generally submissive, kindly, and friendly. An electrode was implanted in the area of her brain called the amygdala. Dr. King stimulated this patient in the amygdala with a current of 4 milliamperes, and there was no observable change in her behavior. (One cannot tell when one's brain is stimulated; there are no receptors that can indicate it, thus, she was unaware of the stimulation.) When the amperage was increased to 5 milliamperes, she became hostile and aggressive. She said such things as "Take my blood pressure. Take it now." Then she said, "If you're going to hold me you'd better get five more men." Whereupon she stood up and started to strike the experimenter. He then wisely turned down the current.

It was possible to turn this woman's anger on and off with a simple flick of the switch because the electrode was located in a part of the neural system for hostility. She indicated having felt anger. She also reported being concerned about the fact that she was angry. She did not report pain or other discomfort. She was simply "turned on" angry. Similar findings have been reported by other investigators (Sem-Jacobsen, 1968; Heath, 1964, pp. 219–244).

There are a number of pathological processes in the human brain that result in the activation of the neural systems for feelings of hostility. Tumors with an irritative focus frequently result in increased irritability and rage attacks if they are located in particular portions of the brain. It is important to note that all brain tumors do not produce pathological aggression. Many, in fact, produce apathy and somnolence. However, if they develop in such a way as to impinge upon and activate the neural systems for aggressive behavior, the syndrome of pathological aggressivity may appear. Tumors in the septal region, the temporal lobe, and the frontal lobe have produced this reaction. In 1962, Sano reported on 1,800 cases of brain tumor and found the irritability syndrome in those that involved the temporal lobe and the anterior hypothalamus.

It is a fortunate fact that in neither humans nor animals is aggression frequent. It is relatively uncommon. Thus, in order to understand the physiology of aggression, we must understand what it is that turns on these neural systems and what it is that turns them off. Perhaps one of the best ways to think about this is in terms of thresholds for the systems. In certain circumstances, the threshold for the firing of the neural systems for aggression is very high. In that case it takes a great deal of provocation to activate them. There are other circumstances in which the threshold is very low and relatively little provocation will result in the activation of the neural systems, with the result that the individual has an increased tendency to behave aggressively.

Some of the variables that influence the thresholds of the neural systems for aggression appear to be hereditary. For example, we have shown in my laboratory that some strains of rats behave aggressively towards small chickens in significantly greater numbers than do other strains (Bandler & Moyer, 1970). It is also possible, as Dr. Lagerspetz of Finland (1964) has shown, to take a large population of mice and select from them the aggressive and nonaggressive animals. Within relatively few generations, if the very aggressive animals are mated, it is possible to develop a highly aggressive strain of mice that will attack immediately when they are put together. If the nonaggressive animals are bred, a strain can be developed that will not fight no matter what you do to them. There is, of course, always a genetic environmental interaction (Barnett, Dickson, & Hocking, 1979). Other recent studies of the inheritance of aggressive behavior include Moss, Watson, Rothery, and Glennie (1982) and Hahn and Haber (1982).

Dr. Wolpy at Earlham College in Indiana tells me that he is raising an extremely aggressive strain of rabbits. These rabbits will attack other rabbits, the experimenter, or hunting dogs. Obviously, we do not have any comparable data on human beings. However, if this model has any validity and if there are specific neural systems for different kinds of aggressive behavior, it must be that different thresholds for aggression are inherited. Neurological differences must be inherited in the same way that differences in the shapes of noses are.

Another significant variable that contributes to differences in the aggression threshold level is blood chemistry. It has been known for centuries that the raging bull can be converted into a gentle steer by castration, which reduces the level of testosterone in the blood stream. The formal work on this problem was done in 1947 by Elizabeth Beeman and has been repeatedly confirmed in many laboratories. Dr. Beeman worked with a strain of mice that fought on being put together. She castrated the animals of the experimental group prior to puberty. After maturity when those mice were put together they did not fight. The control group showed the usual amount of aggression characteristic of that strain. She carried the experiment a step further and implanted pellets of testosterone subcutaneously in the castrated mice. When the testosterone became effective they fought at the same level as the control animals had. She then surgically removed the pellets of testosterone whereupon the mice again became docile. It was possible to manipulate the aggressive behavior of these mice simply by changing their testosterone levels. The role of sex steroids is complex indeed. See Brain (1979, 1980, 1981b) for recent reviews. Some studies have also been done on human wrestlers (Elias, 1981).

There are a variety of other blood chemistry changes that influence the thresholds for aggression. For example, we know that frustration and stress are important variables in inducing aggressive behavior, particularly if the frustration and stress are prolonged. It seems likely that this occurs because the stressors change the hormonal status and thus change the thresholds for the neural systems for aggression. The stress hormones effect different kinds of aggressive behavior differently (Al-Maliki, 1980, pp. 421–426).

It is also true, as many women have found, that there is a period during the week before menstruation when a significant percentage of women feel irritable, hostile, and are easily aroused to anger (Dalton, 1959, 1960, 1961, 1964). Those who have had inadequate training in impulse control sometimes act on those impulses. One study that was conducted on 249 female prison inmates showed that 62% of the crimes of violence were committed in the premenstrual week, whereas only 2% of the crimes of violence were committed in the postmenstrual week (Morton, Addition, Hunt, & Sullivan, 1953).

There appears to be good clinical evidence that a few individuals show an irritable aggression reaction when their blood chemistry is altered by a sudden drop in blood sugar. This is the state of hypoglycemia. At least one controlled study supports the clinical findings. Dr. Ralph Bolton (1973, 1976) spent considerable time with a very hostile tribe of Peruvian Indians, called the Quolla. He hypothesized that the exceptionally high level of social conflict and hostility in the society could be explained, in part, by the tendency toward hypoglycemia among the community residents.

Peer ratings of aggressiveness (which had an acceptable reliability) were studied in relationship to blood sugar levels as determined by a four-hour glucose tolerance test. The aggression ratings were not known to the individuals who read the glucose levels. A chi-square analysis of the data showed a statistically significant relationship between aggression ranking and the change in blood glucose levels during the test. In view of all of the other possible causes of aggressive behavior, this is a remarkable finding and indicates that the relationship must be a powerful one.

Our discussion so far has been concerned with physiology. It should be obvious, however, that learning has an important influence on behavior that we label aggressive just as it does on any other category of behavior. (See O'Nell, 1981, for example.) With the proper use of reward and punishment, an animal can be taught to overeat or to starve to death. By the same method, animals and humans can be taught to exhibit or inhibit their tendencies to hostile behavior. It is clear that aggressive acts that are rewarded have a higher probability of recurring than those that are not. Those that are punished are less likely to occur later.

Human beings, of course, learn better and faster than all other animals. It is therefore reasonable to expect that the internal impulses to aggressive behavior would be more subject to modification by experience in humans than in any other animal. Also, because of the human's ability to manipulate symbols and to substitute one symbol for another, one would expect to find a considerable diversity in the stimuli that will elicit or inhibit activity in the aggression systems. One would also expect that the modes of expression of aggression would be more varied and less stereotyped in humans than in other animals.

It is also important to remember that learned behaviors interact with the internal impulses to aggressive behavior. Thus, an individual who has a very low threshold for the activation of his neural systems for hostility will require more training in impulse control than will other individuals before aggression control will be possible for him.

Some of the most important methods for the control of hostile and antisocial behavior involve training, reeducation, and social change. That is, the external environment is manipulated in some way to alter the individual's behavior or his potential for aggression. However, if this aggression-control model has any validity, it should also be possible to bring about such changes by influencing the internal milieu, by producing changes in the individual's physiology.

I should emphasize at this point that what is possible is certainly not necessarily desirable. I shall discuss what is possible and later will consider some of the profound ethical and moral questions that arise from these therapeutic interventions.

If there are neural systems that are active during, and are responsible for, aggressive behavior, it should be possible to reduce or eliminate aggressive tendencies by interrupting or interfering with those neural systems. There is now abundant evidence that such a procedure is possible. As might be suspected when dealing with neural systems rather than neural centers, there are a number of different brain areas that may be lesioned to delimit aggressive tendencies.

One can take the wild *Lynx rufus rufus*, which will attack with the slightest provocation, and convert it to a pettable pussycat by burning out a very small part of the brain called the amygdala. After the operation the cat will never be violent again (Schreiner & Kling, 1953). The same thing can be done with the wild Norway rat, one of the few animals that will attack without apparent provocation. If a bilateral amygdalectomy is done on this animal, as soon as it comes out of the anesthetic, it will become docile—you can pick it up and carry it around in your lab coat pocket (Woods, 1956). Lesions can also increase aggressive behavior (Bandler & Vergnes, 1979).

Just as there are wild cats and wild monkeys, there are wild people—individuals who have so much spontaneous activity in the neural systems that underlie aggressive behavior that they are a constant threat to themselves and to those around them. These are the relatively few individuals who are confined to the back wards of mental hospitals under either constant sedation or constant restraint. The homicidal hostility of these persons can also be reduced if appropriate brain lesions are made to interrupt the functioning of the systems for irascibility.

There are a number of surgeons who have now performed essentially the same operation on humans as described above for the cat and the rat—a complete or partial bilateral amygdalectomy. The Japanese investigator Narabayashi and his colleagues for example, indicate that they get 85% success in the reduction of violent behavior after a bilateral amygadalectomy (Narabayashi, Nagao, Saito, Yoshido, & Nagahata, 1963). Dr. Heimburger in Indiana claims that he gets a 92% increase in docility in these extremely violent patients through the same operation. Not only was it possible to take those individuals out of isolation and put them in open wards, but two of his patients have been released into society and are adjusting reasonably well (Heimburger, Whitlock, & Kalsbeck, 1966).

There can be no doubt that a number of different brain lesions can reduce the tendency of an individual to both feel and express hostility. That fact is of considerable theoretical significance. It confirms many of the findings on animals and substantiates predictions from the model described above. However, as a practical therapy for the control of aggressive behavior, it leaves much to be desired. There are very few individuals for whom such a drastic approach would be indicated. The most serious problem with the use of lesions for the control of aggression is that the operation is not reversible. Once the lesion is made, nothing can be done to restore the individual to the preoperative state. When the operation is not successful, and it sometimes is not, the patient is brain damaged. It therefore appears clear that surgery should be a last resort therapy and should be used only after all other types of control, both psychological and physiological, have been tried. There is evidence that in some of the hospitals around the world in which aggression control operations are performed, relatively little care is taken to ensure that brain surgery is, indeed, the last resort therapy that it should be (Valenstein, 1973).

The control of aggressive behavior can also be achieved by the activation of those neural systems that send inhibitory fibers to the aggression systems (Albert & Brayley, 1980). Delgado has repeatedly shown that vicious rhesus monkeys can be tamed by the stimulation of aggression suppressor areas (Delgado, 1980).

In order to eliminate the need for restraint and the necessity for connecting wires to the head, a technique was developed by which the brain of the monkey could be stimulated by remote, radio control. The monkey wore a small stimulating device on its back, connected by leads under the skin to electrodes that were implanted in various locations in the brain. The leads were connected through a very small switching relay that could be closed by an impulse from a miniature radio receiver that was bolted to the animal's skull. The radio receiver could be activated by a transmitter some distance away. With this system it was possible to study the monkeys while permitting them to roam free in the caged area (Delgado, 1963, 1981, pp. 82–98).

In one experiment the subject was an aggressive boss monkey that dominated the rest of the colony with his threatening behavior and overt attacks. A radio-controlled electrode was implanted in the monkey's caudate nucleus. When the radio transmitter was activated, the boss monkey received stimulation in the caudate nucleus causing his spontaneous aggressive tendencies to be blocked. His territoriality diminished and the other monkeys in the colony reacted to him differently. They made fewer submissive gestures and showed less fear of him. While the caudate nucleus was being stimulated, it was also possible for the experimenter to enter the cage and catch the monkey.

During one phase of this experiment, the transmitter button was placed inside the cage near the feeding tray and thus made available to all of the monkeys in the colony. One small monkey learned to stand next to the button and watch the boss monkey. Every time the boss would start to threaten and become aggressive the little monkey would push the button and calm him down. I'll leave it to the reader to decide what the political implications of this experiment are. I must say that it's the first experimental evidence I have seen to support St. Matthew's prediction that the meek shall inherit the earth.

Human beings also have neural systems in the brain that when activated function to block ongoing aggressive behavior. Dr. Heath from Tulane has reported on a patient who had an electrode implanted in an area of the brain called the septum. This extremely hostile patient could be brought into the room raging, threatening, swearing, and struggling. When the electrode was connected and the septal region was stimulated (without the patient's knowledge, of course) the patient immediately relaxed, became docile, and assumed a positive attitude. Further, the patient was unable to account for his sudden change in behavior. When the stimulating electrode is in the septal area, the patient may make sexual remarks (Heath, 1955). There are other suppressor areas, however, that do not activate sexually toned responses (Heath, Llewellyn, & Rouchell, 1980). Recently Heath (1977) has reported a significant reduction in pathological violence and aggression in a number of patients after repeated stimulation in the vermal region of the cerebellum.

It would be possible to run a wire from an electrode down the back of a patient's neck to a battery pack that could be worn on the belt. You could then give the patient an "anti-hostility button" and whenever he or she began to feel very mean the button could be pressed in order to calm the patient down.

Heath has already developed the technology to do this in a therapeutic device for an individual with narcolepsy (Heath, 1955). Narcolepsy is a disorder in which the individual falls asleep at inappropriate times. (I have had many students afflicted with this disorder.) Heath's patient's narcolepsy was particularly troublesome because it interfered with his profession. He was a night club entertainer and would sometimes fall asleep in the middle of his act. Dr. Heath implanted an electrode in the arousal system of the patient's brain. A wire was then brought down to a transistorized stimulation unit and the patient was given an "on button." Whenever he started to drift off to sleep the patient could press his "on button" and turn himself back on. He had a type of narcolepsy in which he sometimes fell asleep before he could get to the button. His friends soon learned, however, that when he did that they could reach over and press his "on button" and bring him back into the conversation.

I pointed out that Delgado had his monkey hooked up to a radio. There is no technological reason why the same technique could not be used with humans. At least four people have been reported to have been under radio control of one sort or another (Delgado et al., 1968). An electrode could be placed in a suppressor area of the brain just as Delgado did with the boss monkey. The electrode could be brought out to a radio that is bolted to the subject's head. The brain could then be activated by a transmitter and the patient could move within the area that the transmitter reached.

There are of course some problems with this approach. Since the radio has to be bolted to the skull, it means that the bolts have to go through the scalp. This is a constant possible source of irritation, as well as a source of infection. There are also psychological problems— people are likely to feel conspicuous with radios on their heads.

Even those problems are being solved by the recent developments in microminiaturization in electronics. It is now possible to take the radio, the power to operate it, and a radio transmitter that will send out brain waves and put them all into a unit about the size and shape of a half dollar. The electrode can be attached to this unit, which can be implanted under the skin anywhere. As soon as the individual's hair grows back the implant is unnoticeable. In fact, it is technologically possible right now, that the next person you meet on the street will be under radio control and you will not know it unless his or her hair is parted wrong.

The suppression of aggression by electrical stimulation is, I think, of considerable theoretical importance. We know that humans possess these neural suppressor systems and we are gradually learning many of the characteristics of suppression mechanisms. However, like brain lesions, this is not yet a reasonable or a generally useful therapeutic technique. The surgical risk of electrode implants is even lower than that of stereotaxic brain lesions and can be considered negligible. There are, however, other serious side effects that merit a great deal more research before electrical stimulation of the brain of humans can be considered risk free. Although there are no data on humans, it has been shown in mice, rats, cats, and monkeys that repeated, brief, subthreshold stimulation of the amygdala results in a progressive lowering of seizure threshold and ultimately of behavioral convulsions. This increase in seizure potential resulting from brain stimulation has been referred to as the kindling effect. Goddard (1972, pp. 581–596) who has studied this phenomenon in some detail, concludes that the kindling effect is a relatively permanent transynaptic change resulting from the stimulation. It is not due to tissue damage or scar formation.

It may someday be possible to circumvent the kindling effect. Until then, however, any procedure that involves repeated electrical stimulation of the human brain places the patient at risk.

The physiological model of aggressive behavior indicates that the neurological systems for aggressive behavior are sensitized by chemical factors in the blood stream. These are primarily but not exclusively hormones. An understanding of the endocrinology and blood chemistry influences on aggression should ultimately lead to a rational therapy for certain kinds of hostility in humans. The woman, for example, who suffers from periodic hyper-irritability every month, has a physician who either isn't aware of the problem or doesn't keep up on the literature. There are a variety of therapeutic measures now that can be taken to alleviate that problem.

There are also people who show a kind of aggressive behavior known as sex-related aggression. These are the violent individuals for whom the object of aggression is the same as the object for sexual behavior. These are the individuals who commit brutal sexual murders, for example.

Aggressive behavior that is directly associated with sexual behavior, either heterosexual or homosexual, can most generally be controlled by reducing or blocking the androgens in the blood stream. The simplest and most obvious method of accomplishing this is by castration. There is now considerable evidence that this operative procedure is effective in reducing levels of sexual arousal regardless of its orientation. This is a drastic therapy and there are obvious problems with it. It is permanent and irreversible. There are also a variety of physical and psychological side effects. However, it has been offered to sex criminals as an alternative to prison in some countries (Bremer, 1959).

More recently some investigators have attempted to block the effects of the male hormone by giving estrogenic or progestogenic hormones or antiandrogenic drugs. Although a great deal more work needs to be done and the problem of side effects must be considered, these techniques do show promise (Chatz, 1972; Blumer & Migeon, Note 1).

It seems clear that the techniques for physiological intervention outlined above should not be rejected out of hand. However, the moral and ethical implications of those techniques should be carefully considered. (See papers from the International Society for Research on Aggression Symposium on Ethics, 1981, i.e., Adams, 1981; Brain, 1981a; Genoves, 1981; Wikler, 1981.) The following case brings some of those problems into focus.

> An individual, Mr. J., went to the violence clinic of the Massachusetts General Hospital in Boston. He checked in because of his tendency to fly into rages over relatively minor incidents. His recent behavior increased his concern because his aggressive tendencies were, at times, directed toward his family. Diagnostic techniques revealed that he had some spontaneous firing of an epileptoid nature in the temporal lobe. That dysfunction has been associated with violent tendencies. Mr. J. was accepted as a patient. Further diagnosis included the implementation of a large number of electrodes directed toward the region of the amygdala. The electrodes were used for stimulating and recording to determine the precise area producing the spontaneous epileptoid activity. That area could then be lesioned resulting in an alleviation of the symptoms. One morning after most of the diagnostic procedures had been completed, the patient told the nurses that he planned to leave the hospital, find his wife and kill her. He would not be dissuaded. Dr. Ervin was called in and was able to convince Mr. J. to have just a few more tests. In the testing room, an area of the brain was stimulated that had been previously determined as being an aggression suppression area. The patient responded with an immediate reduction in hostile thoughts and behavior. His attitude toward his wife also changed. He no longer wanted to kill her and was most grateful for the stimulators that had changed his feelings. In that state of mind, he readily agreed

to sign the informed consent form to give permission for the operation (a small brain lesion in the temporal lobe). The surgery was scheduled for the following morning. (Ervin, Note 2)

On awakening and being reminded of the operation, Mr. J. responded indignantly that no one was going to burn anything out of his brain.

A question that must be considered is, "Did the patient give an informed consent?" And did he give an informed rejection of his earlier agreement? At a more philosophical level, "When was the patient exercising his own free will?" I do not know the answers, but perhaps exploring these kinds of questions will yield answers in the future.

Reference Notes

1. Blumer, D., & Migeon, C. *Treatment of impulsive behavior disorders in males with medroxyprogesterone acetate.* Paper presented at the annual meeting of the American Psychiatric Association, May 1973.
2. Ervin, F. Personal communication, 1973.

References

Adams, D. B. Ethics of aggression research: Papers from a symposium of International Society for Research on Aggression. *Aggressive Behavior*, 1981, 7, 367–370.

Al-Maliki, S. Influences of stress-related hormones on a variety of models of attack behaviour in laboratory mice. In P. S. McConnell, G. J. Boer, H. J. Romijn, N. E. van de Poll, & M. A. Corner (Eds.), *Progress in brain research* (Vol. 53). Amsterdam: Elsevier North-Holland Biomedical Press, 1980.

Albert, D. J., & Brayley, K. N. Mouse killing by rats: Suppression by electrical stimulation ventral to the anterior septum. *Aggressive Behavior*, 1980, 6, 31–36.

Bandler, R. Predatory attack behavior in the cat elicited by preoptic region stimulation: A comparison with behavior elicited by hypothalmic and midbrain stimulation. *Aggressive Behavior*, 1979, 5, 269–282.

Bandler, R., & Fatouris, D. Centrally elicited behavior in cats: Post-stimulus excitability and mid-brain-hyphthalmic inter-relationships. *Brain Research*, 1978, 153, 427–433.

Bandler, R., Halliday, R., & Abeyewardene, S. Centrally-elicited aggressive behavior in the cat: A changing view. In M. Girgis & L. G. Kiloh (Eds.), *Limbic epilepsy and the dyscontrol syndrome*. Amsterdam: Elsevier North-Holland Biomedical Press, 1980.

Bandler, R. J., & Moyer, K. E. Animals spontaneously attacked by rats. *Communications in Behavioral Biology*, 1970, 5, 177–182.

Bandler, R., & Vergnes, M. Interspecies aggression in the rat: The role of the diagonal band of broca. *Brain Research*, 1979, 175, 327–333.

Barnett, S. A., Dickson, R. G., & Hocking, W. E. Genotype and environment in the social interactions of wild and domestic "Norway" rats. *Aggressive Behavior*, 1979, 5, 105–119.

Beeman, E. A. The effect of male hormone on aggressive behavior in mice. *Physiological Zoology*, 1947, 20, 373–405.

Bolton, R. Hostility in fantasy: A further test of the hypoglycemia-aggression hypothesis. *Aggressive Behavior*, 1976, 2, 257–274.

Bolton, R. Aggression and hypoglycemia among the Qolla: A study in psychobiological anthropology. *Ethnology,* 1973, *12,* 227–257.

Brain, P. F. *Hormones, drugs, and aggression: Vol. 3. Annual research reviews.* Montreal: Eden Press, 1979.

Brain, P. F. Adaptive aspects of hormonal correlates of attack and defence in laboratory mice: A study in ethobiology. In P. S. McConnell, G. J. Boer, H. J. Romijn, N. E. van de Poll, & M. A. Corner (Eds.), *Progress in Brain Research* (Vol. 53). Amsterdam: Elsevier North-Holland Biomedical Press, 1980.

Brain, P. F. Diverse action of hormones on aggression in animals and man. In L. Valzelli & L. Morgese (Eds.), *Aggression and violence: A psycho/biological and clinical approach.* Milano, Italy: Edizioni Saint Vincent, 1981a.

Brain, P. F. The use of animals in aggression research. *Aggressive Behavior,* 1981b, *7,* 383–388.

Bremer, J. *Asexualization.* New York: MacMillan, 1959.

Chatz, T. L. Management of the male adolescent sex offenders. *International Journal of Offender Therapy,* 1972, *2,* 109–115.

Dalton, K. Menstruation and acute psychiatric illness. *British Medical Journal,* 1959, *1,* 148–149.

Dalton, K. Schoolgirls' misbehavior and menstruation. *British Medical Journal,* 1960, *2,* 1647.

Dalton, K. Menstruation and crime. *British Medical Journal,* 1961, *3,* 1752–1753.

Dalton, K. *The premenstrual syndrome.* Springfield, IL: Charles C Thomas, 1964.

Delgado, J. M. R. Cerebral heterostimulation in a monkey colony. *Science,* 1963, *141,* 161–163.

Delgado, J. M. R. Brain stimulation and neurochemical studies on the control of aggression. In Proceedings of N.A.T.O. Advanced Study Institute on *The biology of aggression,* Bonas, France, July 1980. Wilhelminalaan, Holland: Sijthoff & Noordhoff, 1980.

Delgado, J. M. R. Neuronal constellations in aggressive behavior. In L. Vazelli & L. Morgese (Eds.), *Aggression and violence: a psycho/biological and clinical approach.* Milano, Italy: Edizioni Saint Vincent, 1981.

Delgado, J. M. R., Mark, V., Sweet, W., Ervin, F., Weiss, G., Bach-Y-Rita, G., & Hagiwara, R. Intracerebral radio stimulation and recording in completely free patients. *Journal of Nervous and Mental Diseases,* 1968, *147,* 329–340.

Egger, M. D., & Flynn, J. P. Effect of electrical stimulation of the amygdala on hypothalamically elicited attack behavior in cats. *Journal of Neurophysiology,* 1963, *26,* 705–720.

Elias, M. Serum cortisol, testosterone and testosterone-binding globulin responses to competitive fighting in human males. *Aggressive Behavior,* 1981, *7,* 215–224.

Fuchs, S. A. G., Dalsass, M., Siegel, H. E., & Siegel, A. The neural pathways mediating quiet-biting attack behavior from the hypothalmus in the cat: A functional autoradiographic study. *Aggressive Behavior,* 1981, *7,* 51–68.

Genoves, S. The dissemination of information and misinformation on aggression to the public. *Aggressive Behavior,* 1981, *7,* 371–376.

Goddard, G. V. Long term alteration following amygdaloid stimulation. In B. Eleftheriou (Ed.), *The neurobiology of the amygdala.* New York: Plenum Press, 1972.

Hahn, M. E., & Haber, S. B. The inheritance of agonistic behavior in male mice: A diallel analysis. *Aggressive Behavior,* 1982, *8,* 19–38.

Heath, R. G. Correlations between levels of psychological awareness and physiological activity in the central nervous system. *Psychosomatic Medicine,* 1955, *17,* 383–395.

Heath, R. G. Pleasure response of human subjects to direct stimulation of the brain: Physiologic and psychodynamic considerations. In R. G. Heath (Ed.), *The role of pleasure in behavior.* New York: Harper & Row, 1964.

Heath, R. G. Modulation of emotion with a brain pacemaker: Treatment for intractable psychiatric illness. *Journal of Nervous and Mental Disease,* 1977, *165,* 300–317.

Heath, R. G. The neural basis for violent behavior: Physiology and anatomy. In L. Valzelli & L. Morgese (Eds.), *Aggression and violence: A psycho/biological and clinical approach.* Milano, Italy: Edizioni Saint Vincent, 1981.

Heath, R. G., Llewellyn, R. C., & Rouchell, A. M. The cerebellar pacemaker for intractable behavioral disoders and epilepsy: Follow-up reports. *Biological Psychiatry,* 1980, *15,* 243–256.

Heimburger, R. F., Whitlock, C. C., & Kalsbeck, J. E. Stereotaxic amygdalotomy for epilepsy with aggressive behavior. *Journal of the American Medical Association,* 1966, *198,* 165–169.

King, H. E. Psychological effects of excitation in the limbic system. In D. E. Sheer (Ed.), *Electrical stimulation of the brain.* Austin: University of Texas Press, 1961.

Kruk, M. R., & Van der Poel, A. M. Is there evidence for a neural correlation of an aggressive behavioural system in the hypothalamus of the rat? In P. S. McConnell, G. J. Boer, H. J. Romijn, N. E. van de Poll, & M. A. Corner (Eds.), *Progress in brain research* (Vol. 53). Amsterdam: Elsevier North-Holland Biomedical Press, 1980.

Kruk, M. R., Van der Poel, A. M., & de Vos-Frerichs, T. P. The induction of aggressive behaviour by electrical stimulation in the hypothalamus of male rats. *Behaviour,* 1979, *70,* 292–322.

Lagerspetz, K. Studies on the aggressive behavior of mice. *Annales Academiae Scientiarum Fennicae,* 1964, Series B. *131,* 1–131.

Morton, J. H., Addition, R. G., Hunt, L., & Sullivan, J. J. A clinical study of premenstrual tension. *American Journal of Obstetrics & Gynecology,* 1953, *65,* 1182–1191.

Moss, R., Watson, A., Rothery, P., & Glennie, W. Inheritance of dominance and aggressiveness in captive red grouse *Lagopus lagopus scoticus. Aggressive Behavior,* 1982, *8,* 1–18.

Moyer, K. E. Kinds of aggression and their physiological basis. *Communications in Behavioral Biology,* 1968, *2,* 65–87.

Moyer, K. E. *The psychobiology of aggression.* New York: Harper & Row, 1976.

Narabayashi, H., Nagao, T., Saito, Y., Yoshido, M., & Nagahata, M. Stereotaxic amygdalotomy for behavior disorders. *Archives of Neurology,* 1963, *9,* 1016.

O'Nell, C. W. Hostility management and the control of aggression in a Zapotec community. *Aggressive Behavior,* 1981, *7,* 351–366.

Robinson, B. W., Alexander, M., & Bowne, G. Dominance reversal resulting from aggressive responses evoked by brain telestimulation. *Physiology and Behavior,* 1969, *4,* 749–752.

Sano, K. Sedative neorosurgery: With special reference to postero-medial hypothalamotomy. *Neurologia Medico-Chirurgica,* 1962, *4,* 112–142.

Schreiner, L., & Kling, A. Behavioral changes following rhinencephalic injury in cat. *Journal of Neurophysiology,* 1953, *16,* 643–658.

Sem-Jacobson, C. W. *Depth-electrographic stimulation of the human brain and behavior.* Springfield, IL: Charles C Thomas, 1968.

Valenstein, E. S. *Brain Control.* New York: Wiley, 1973.

Wikler, D. Ethics: As theory and as practice. *Aggressive Behavior,* 1981, *7,* 377–382.

Woods, J. W. "Taming" of the wild Norway rat by rhinencephalic lesions. *Nature,* 1956, *178,* 869.

COMMENTS

Few students take the first course in psychology in order to learn about its physiological aspects. Many expect physiology to be boring. Thus, the motivational function of a good lecture becomes especially important. To begin his lecture, Moyer gives his views on the effective employment and the abuses of the lecture method. Humor enlivens the lecture, but dramatic cases such as those offered by Moyer are even more stimulating—Flynn's work on hostile cats, for example. The point is made even more vivid by the example of King's angry patient, who demands to have her blood pressure taken.

I have found the lecture quite helpful for clarifying information. For example, a very general review of functional neuroanatomy is necessary to provide a context of physiological research. As part of this review, it is important to help students understand that the amygdala is not a center for aggression but part of a biochemical neural system. Slides are useful for this purpose. (A good teacher, of course, learns to use a projector and checks the orientation of the slides before class.) Any introductory text can be supplemented by material on the nervous system. Moyer has made effective use of the beautiful drawings of Frank Netter (1958), for example.

The methodology of physiological psychology can also be clarified by a lecture that includes not only slides but actual demonstrations. What are the various ways of stimulating and lesioning the brain? Show students a stereotaxic instrument, but be alert for queasiness if you put a rat in it. The most effective and dramatic classroom demonstration I have ever used involved a specially prepared Skinner box, which allowed students to view a rat pressing a bar in order to receive electrical stimulation of the septal region.[1] A red light on the side of the box indicated when a shock was delivered following a bar press. I could turn the rat on with two or three externally presented stimulations. The animal then pressed the bar vigorously for a couple of minutes. With a flourish I turned off the shock—and the rat.

Such a demonstration is not necessary, however, to get students to think and ask questions about the extent to which we can generalize from animals to humans or to consider the ethical issues related to research in this area. Many will have read enough science fiction to recognize the potential implications of these findings. A teacher can both feed that speculation and bring it back to reality (Valenstein, 1973). After your inspiring lecture and an enthusiastic discussion,

---

[1]This box was obtained from Alan Fisher's laboratory at the University of Pittsburgh. I do not know where to obtain it now.

your students may discover that physiological psychology is one of the most interesting areas they have studied.

Some of the questions from the audience following Moyer's lecture were about basic processes. The bearing that sensory input has on aggressive behavior was discussed, citing the work of Flynn. Cognitive processes play a role also. For example, Moyer pointed out that an intervention may be directed toward helping a person reinterpret targets of aggression. (The police are not coming after you.)

Could an entire population be controlled using physiological methods, wondered one member of the audience, and who would want to do that? Moyer doubted that anyone wanting to control masses of people would use such inefficient methods. The logistics of mass implants are too complex. He reminded us that Hitler mobilized millions for aggressive purposes using methods based on social psychology.

Finally, the question was asked, "Who will control the controllers?" Are the people who are doing research on aggression asking this question? Yes, they are, but they have found no answers. Controlling the controllers is obviously an issue of great importance to our futures and to the achievement of world peace.

References

Netter, F. H., *The Ciba collection of medical illustrations: Vol. I. Nervous system.* New York: Ciba Pharmaceutical Products Inc., 1958.

Valenstein, E. S., *Brain control.* New York: Wiley, 1973.

ROCHEL GELMAN

RECENT TRENDS IN COGNITIVE DEVELOPMENT

R ochel Gelman has been a professor of psychology at the University of Pennsylvania since 1968. She received her doctorate from UCLA in 1967. She is a member of the Board of Cognitive Psychology and a fellow of Division 7 of the American Psychological Association (APA). She held a John S. Guggenheim Fellowship, was a fellow at the Center for Advanced Study in the Behavioral Sciences, and received an APA Early Career Contribution Award. Recently she taught cognitive development at the Institute of Psychology in China.

Gelman's work has focused on the nature and development of concepts. She has done research on numerical knowledge, communication skills, logical thought, causal reasoning, and the nature of learning in development. In her doctoral thesis she proposed that preschool children fail the Piagetian conservation task not because they lack the underlying competence but because they attend to the wrong features. Since then she has gone on to uncover many cognitive competencies of young children. Although she now considers herself a structuralist and is sympathetic with many of Piaget's notions about development, she maintains that the stage theory is not supported. Rather she suggests that different structures mediate different domains of cognition.

RECENT TRENDS IN COGNITIVE DEVELOPMENT

My goal in this paper is to bring you to the view that the study of cognitive development informs our understanding of the nature of the mind. This position was Piaget's and, although his work has been the subject of much criticism, scrutiny, and debate, on this matter he was right.

The plan of this paper is as follows. I will first go over some old and some new facts about cognitive development. These seemingly contradictory facts lead me to a lengthy treatment of one predominant trend in the current study of cognitive development—the study of structures that are invariant throughout development. Such work highlights how developmental work uncovers facts about universals of cognition. It also provides new insights into what does develop. Next, I turn to the question of how development might proceed. Finally, I summarize what I think are the major trends in cognitive

This essay was presented as a lecture in the 1982 G. Stanley Hall Lecture Series at the annual meeting of the American Psychological Association, Washington, DC. Preparation of this talk was supported by NSF Grant BNS-8140573 to Rochel Gelman and a Sloan Foundation grant to the Program in Cognitive Science at the University of Pennsylvania. I thank Anne Fowler, C. R. Gallistel, and Elizabeth Spelke for helpful comments on an earlier version of this paper.

development. The major points that arise from my discussion are these:

1. There are many cognitive capacities at a very early age that probably serve to guide development.

2. Most cognitive development is self-motivated.

3. The path of cognitive development is multifaceted and includes (a) increased control over performance constraints, (b) development of access and metacognition, (c) inductions of new principles, (d) construction of knowledge systems, and (e) differentiation and integration of structures and concepts.

Cognitive Development:
Old and New Facts

Two of Piaget's best known findings are those about the development of the object concept in infancy and conservation in middle childhood. Piaget found that acquisition of the object concept seems to pass through six stages, taking about 2 years to do so. During stages 1 and 2 (0–4 months), infants stop attending once objects leave their immediate line of sight. During stage 3 (about 4–8 months) infants reach for and grasp visible objects, follow objects as they fall on the floor, and even anticipate their trajectories. But, incredibly, they stop reaching for or looking at an object if that object disappears behind a barrier. An object that once grabbed their attention no longer has any effect on them. It's as if an object is "out of sight, out of mind," as Piaget concluded.

During stage 4 (about 8–12 months) infants will search for and retrieve an object they see someone cover; however, they show a bizarre tendency. If that object is removed from behind the barrier (A) and, *while the baby watches,* is moved behind another barrier (B), the baby searches only behind the first barrier! The infant seems not to realize it is the same object: "The object is still not the same to the child as it is to us: a substantial body, individualized and displaced in space without depending on the action context in which it was inserted" (Piaget, 1954, p. 64).

In stage 5 (12–18 months), despite the fact that children search for the object in that place to which they saw it moved, they do not search for an object that is invisibly moved to another hiding place. They do not seem to believe that the attractive object "has just got to be somewhere." This, Piaget maintained, requires an ability to use symbols to represent the object—an ability that he concluded does not reveal itself until the end of sensorimotor intelligence or stage 6.

The conservation findings are similarly surprising. In the number conservation task, children between the ages of 4 and 7 years are shown two rows of objects lined up in one-to-one correspondence.

Having answered correctly that both rows have the same number, they watch as the experimenter transforms one of the rows, usually making it longer or shorter than the other. Once again the child is asked whether both rows have the same number of objects. Children of 6 or 7 years quickly say they do and readily explain why: "You didn't add or subtract any" or "You just pushed them around." In dramatic contrast, the younger child denies the continued equivalence, and claims one row has more than the other. For Piaget this meant that young children believe transformations that alter perceptual features of a quantitative display actually alter the amount therein. In order not to believe this the child is said to have to advance to the stage of concrete operational thought, a stage characterized in terms of the availability of certain mathematical and logical structures. (See Flavell, 1963; Ginsburg & Opper, 1979; or Gruber & Vonèche, 1977 for details).

These are reliable findings, so much so that I always invite my introductory psychology students to confirm them with children they know. However, when different tasks that clearly test for the same or related abilities are used, different conclusions about the nature of the child's capacities and concepts are reached. Baillargeon's study on the object concept in 5-month-old babies and Gelman and Gallistel's study on preschooler's understanding of number illustrate different conclusions that have been reached.

Baillargeon (Note 1) worked with a procedure commonly used with infants—habituation. Infants were shown a screen that rotated forward and backward through an arc of 180°. As expected, infants who first watched attentively became bored, as evidenced by a 50% drop in their looking times. Once habituation occurred, a yellow cube was placed alongside the screen for two trials of viewing. Then the cube was placed behind the screen and on alternating trials the infant saw a screen that once again rotated through a 180° arc (and at least from the adult perspective seemed to crush the covered object) or a 120° arc, as would be required by the presence of a solid object behind the screen. One-way mirrors and variations in lighting created the visual effects. Despite the fact that infants habituated to the 180° rotation, they now looked longer at it than at the 120° rotation. Why would they do so unless they knew that there was supposed to be a solid three-dimensional object behind the screen and hence were taken aback by seeing the screen rotating through it? Five-month-old babies must believe that objects have permanence—and solidity as well (cf. Locke's definition of the object concept).

I (1978) investigated preschoolers' understanding of number. To assess children's understanding of the role of various transformations, such as lengthening or adding, on the cardinal value of a set, we used a variation on the magic show. In phase 1, our version of the magician's setup, children were shown two plates, each with a different number of objects on them, for example, two versus three toy green mice. Without mentioning number, we told the children that one of the plates was the "winner" and the other the "loser" and that every time they found the winner-plate they would get a prize. Each child and the experimenter were to take turns either covering up or shuffling the covered plates, after which the child could guess which can contained the winner and then to look and see if he or she was right. Each correct identification was rewarded. In fact, children seldom erred. Because children said that a plate was the winner or loser because of the numerical value therein—"It wins cuz it has three—one, two, three"—we knew they had responded on the basis of number.

Unknown to the child, phase 2 of the experiment started with the experimenter making surreptitious changes in the displays. Depending on the condition and the experiment, a child encountered the effects of adding or subtracting one or more items from a display, such as spreading out a row and making it longer or substituting a different colored or even different type of item. In most experiments small set sizes ($N<6$) were used.

The results were straightforward. Those children who encountered irrelevant changes deemed them such; those who encountered relevant transformations pronounced them relevant. Thus changes in number elicited considerable surprise: "Eeee, how did that happen?!" Furthermore, the children postulated the relevant transformation: "One gone—Jesus Christ came and took it." They also told us what number they expected and what number they actually encountered. Children in the number-irrelevant conditions as often as not noted the change. When they did, they said it did not matter because the numbers were as expected: "Still three, they just spreaded out." This was even true when the color or the type of object changed.

What can be said of such contradictory findings? To infants, at least, we have to grant that their conception of the world is much more accurate than Piaget, or anyone else for that matter, once thought (cf. Gibson, 1982). Still, it will not do to say we can ignore Piaget; his results are too reliable and too compelling. What we need is a theory that can incorporate the old and the new. The recognition of this state of affairs has created an atmosphere of excitement and theoretical ferment.

What Does Not, What Does Develop

One clear focus of research in cognitive development in the last decade has been the search for mental structures that do not develop. The strategy has been to compare and contrast children of different ages. This has yielded new insights on the nature of what does develop in particular and on the nature of the human mind in general. To illustrate, I will discuss at length some of the recent work that has been done on classification abilities. A briefer treatment of number and causality will follow.

Classification

Traditional Findings

Piaget's account of the conservation failures of preschoolers uses a stage theory in which children acquire new and qualitatively different mental structures at different points in development. The preschooler is said to lack the concrete operations of classification and ordering structures—structures that are presumed to mediate the ability to solve classification and seriation tasks, and, when classification and seriation tasks are integrated, conservation tasks.

To buttress the conclusion that preschoolers lack concrete operational structures, Piaget pointed to the development of classification abilities, noting the preschooler's inability to consistently apply a taxonomic classification scheme or to make inferences about hierarchical relationships (Inhelder & Piaget, 1964). Similar ineptitudes have been reported by Bruner and Olver (1963), Vygotsky (1962), and Werner (1940). Indeed, the young child's difficulty with classification stands as one of the best documented facts in cognitive development. Rather than use consistent criteria to classify, children organize thematically—they put objects together that make up a building, remind them of a given setting, tell a story, and so forth. Suppose young children were shown pictures of various children, adults, cars, and bicycles. It is a safe assumption that they would put the children with the bicycles and the adults with the cars. In contrast, older children and adults can be expected to put all the people in one pile and all the vehicles in another.

Another aspect of preschoolers' classification schemes is illustrated by their performance on the Piagetian class-inclusion task. When shown a display made up of two different kinds of fruit and asked, "Which has more, the fruit or the apples?" they say, "The apples." They fail to compare the subordinate class with the superordinate class. Despite the robustness of the results on various classification tasks, as I will show in the discussion that follows, it is no longer possible to interpret these results to mean that young children lack the capacity to impose hierarchical organization.

Ontological Knowledge

Keil (1979) provides compelling evidence for the view that an adult's ontological knowledge (knowledge about the basic categories of existence) is hierarchically organized and may be innately constrained. It seems that what objects we know and what we know about them—hence, which predicates we can use when describing them or thinking about them—are organized in a strict hierarchy.

To discover the way we organize ontological knowledge, Keil asked subjects in one experiment to judge what could or could not be predicated about an object. For example, students were asked if it was correct to say, "The lady is not sorry," "The day is an hour long," "The day is heavy," and so on. The choice of sentences was determined by Keil's theory of how we organize our knowledge about ontological categories. This is illustrated in Figure 1 in what Keil calls (following the philosopher Sommers, 1965) a predicability tree. Words in uppercase letters stand for predicates that are true (or not true) of the objects that are shown in lowercase letters. The solid line branches represent categories and subcategories of predicates; the dotted lines represent categories and subcategories of objects. Objects and predicates are organized in a strict hierarchy. Starting at the bottom, people and animals are classified separately as regards the predicates "is honest" and "is sorry." People and animals are classified together but separately from plants as regards the predicates "is asleep" and "is hungry." Moving up the hierarchy, all living things are classified together and separate from all inanimate things, and so on.

This particular predicability tree is more than theoretical. It conforms to how subjects judged the sentences they were given. Hence subjects said that it was all right to say that a man, a pig, a tree, a car, some milk, a storm, and a story can be thought about. However, subjects maintained that events like storms cannot be red or heavy; physical objects can. They also said that only animate objects can be said to be dead, able to breathe, and so forth. This is wonderful evidence that knowledge is hierarchically organized. Interestingly, the same results were obtained cross-culturally.

Keil[1] also found that at least by 3 years of age (the youngest children he has tested), children have predicability trees that are hierarchically organized along the same lines. It is true that 3-year-olds do not have as richly differentiated an understanding about objects in the world as adults do. But their knowledge can be mapped onto the adult predicability tree by simply collapsing some of the nodes in the adult tree. Thus where adults distinguish between plants, animals,

[1] There is some recent evidence to suggest that Keil's ontological categories work better for knowledge about objects than for knowledge about events (Mandler, 1983).

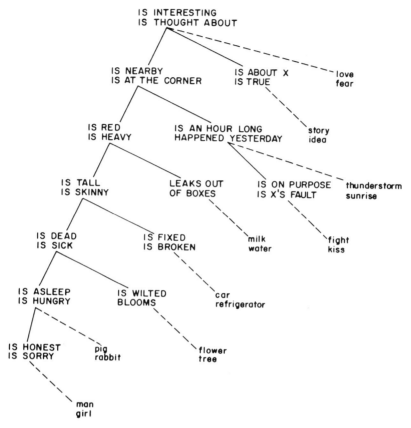

Figure 1. An example of a predictability tree developed by Keil (1979). Reprinted by permission.

and people on the one hand, and natural objects versus artifacts on the other hand, 3-year-olds distinguish only animate objects from inanimate objects. So the child may say that trees can be sorry, but that cars cannot. With development, the child's knowledge of subcategories is differentiated out of the larger categories.

In the last 2 years there has been a spate of other evidence that preschoolers have a hierarchical classification scheme. (See Clark, 1983; Gelman & Baillargeon, 1983; Markman & Callahan, in press; Mandler, 1983, for reviews.) Gelman and Spelke (1981) conclude that what evidence there is supports an innate ability to treat animate and inanimate objects differently. Keil's (1981) conclusion that the development of ontological knowledge is governed by an innate hierarchical organization constraint may be right.

Some Reasons for Failure to Classify

If young children have the capacity to use a hierarchical organization scheme, why do they fail to do so in the tasks used by Piaget, Vygotsky, and Werner?

The Role of Knowledge

Given that the ontological trees of very young children are not as differentiated as those of adults, it is clear that young children simply know less than adults about the nature of objects in the world. Perhaps this is why children fail to employ a classification scheme. As it happens, there are 4-year-olds in this country who have a passion for learning about dinosaurs and hence provide a test of this hypothesis. Chi and Koeske (1983) have done an in-depth study of one such child in Pittsburgh. When asked to recall the names of the dinosaurs that he knew, the child came back with a list that was hierarchically organized by some very abstract criteria, such as whether or not the dinosaurs were land-living or meat-eating.

Competition From Other Structures

Although young children's limited knowledge-base is surely a factor in their tendency not to classify consistently on the basis of superordinate criteria, it cannot be the only problem. This is because many studies do present children with familiar materials. Recent research makes clear that the failure of young children to use classification is due partly to their preference for other modes of organization.

Collections. Markman (1981) distinguishes between concepts organized as classes and those organized as collections. The difference between the concepts of trees and forests illustrates the distinction. Given a particular tree, one can answer whether or not it is a member of the class trees. However, given the same instance of the same tree, one cannot answer whether it is a member of a forest. There must be other trees nearby; the instance tree is a member of a forest only if it is in proximity to a large number of other trees. Likewise, a particular child can be said to be a member of the class people. But unless one knows that the child has a parent (or other relation) one cannot determine whether that child is a member of the collection family. Markman contends that class terms focus attention on the particular members of a display, collection terms on the totality of the display. Hence, she concluded that young children might be better able to keep in mind the whole of a display when thinking about a part in terms of a collection rather than in terms of a class. Her research suggests that this is so.

Markman and Siebert (1976) tested children with both collection and class terms. As an illustration, when children were in the collection condition they were asked, "Who would have more toys to play with, someone who owned the blue blocks or someone who owned the pile?" When in the class condition they were asked, "Who would have more toys to play with, someone who owned the blue blocks or someone who owned the blocks?" This simple change in wording—notice that the stimuli were identical for the two conditions—produced dramatic differences in the child's ability to indicate that the whole contained more than its subcategories.

There is evidence that children—and adults, if you accept the idea that teenagers are adults—impose a collection organization in a situation where it would seem they would have to impose a class-inclusion one (Markman, Horton, & McLanahan, 1980). For example, Markman et al. tried to teach subjects novel class-inclusion hierarchies. Subjects were taught that one subset (A) of novel figures were "zugs," another subset (B) were "laks," and that all of the figures together (C) were "bivs." Then they were tested to determine whether they represented their knowledge in a class-inclusion hierarchy, for example, if they knew an individual zug was also a biv. They did not. Pupils as old as 14 years of age denied that any single element was a biv, and picked up several zugs and laks when asked for a biv. This is akin to denying that a rose or a petunia is a flower and behaving as if a flower was a bouquet—hence the handful of objects when asked for one! In other words, subjects imposed a collection organization rather than a class organization on the materials that were organized (from the experimenter's point of view) in a class-inclusion hierarchy. Such results highlight the fact that part of the reason young children fail to use a class-inclusion scheme is that there are other structural tendencies dominating their minds.

Schemas. Jean Mandler (1981) has proposed that there are yet other modes of conceptual organization that compete with and often override the use of classification. These are organizations based on spatiotemporal relations as opposed to class relations. The fundamental units in these types of organization are not categories but schemas. These have been shown to represent our everyday knowledge of classes of events like restaurant-going; our knowledge of faces; our knowledge of rooms in general and kitchens, bedrooms, and bathrooms in particular; our knowledge of folktales and story grammars; and so forth (Bartlett, 1932; Bower, Black, & Turner, 1979; Bransford, 1979; Mandler & Parker, 1976; Rumelhart & Ortony, 1977; Schank & Abelson, 1977; Stein & Trabasso, 1982).

The evidence that adults use structures that capitalize on spatial or temporal relations is extensive. For example, we retain a general script for restaurant-going and hence can make inferences about less than complete accounts of activities in a restaurant. Thus, even if I were not told that a waiter took orders before removing menus from people's plates, I would still be able to say this was so. Correctly or not, I would infer it from my restaurant script. The fact that we have a schema for a room will lead us to misremember a scene that shows chairs on walls; we normalize our memory to place them on floors where they belong (Biederman, 1982; Mandler & Parker, 1976). Our use of story grammars often underlies our falsely remembering material that was not in fact in a given story, introduces intrusions in our recall, alters the order of input toward the canonical form dictated by the underlying grammar of the story, and leads us to summarize for gist (Mandler, 1983; Stein & Trabasso, 1982).

Recall the example of the preschooler who put pictures of children with pictures of bicycles and pictures of adults with pictures of cars. Rather than saying the child lacks a classification structure we could say the child took the opportunity to use scripts about who uses what forms of transportation. To support this line of argument, it is necessary to show that preschoolers do indeed share adults' predilection to form event schemata and, when given a choice, use them as opposed to classification structures. Evidence supporting the use of either schema is available.

Nelson and her students (Nelson & Gruendel, 1981) found that children as young as 3 years have well-ordered scripts for a variety of the classes of events that make up parts of their lives, including restaurant-going (especially to McDonalds) and lunch at school. And they, like adults, misremember the order in which they recall because of a powerful tendency to make the input conform to canonical order. Mandler, Bates, Gerard, & O'Connell (cited in Mandler, Note 2) are now finding evidence for the presence of event schemata in 1½- to 2-year-olds. Toddlers were asked to imitate event sequences that were well ordered, reversed, or incorrect. An example of a well-ordered sequence was a teddy bear placed in a tub, then washed, and then dried. The children did best on the well-ordered sequences and, most significantly, reordered other sequences to conform to a canonical order.

The work on story grammars adds weight to the conclusion that event schemata are available to young children. Poulson, Kintsch, Kintsch, and Premack (1979) found that 4-year-olds used a story schema to "read" a series of pictures. Mandler and Johnson (1977) found that children, like adults, invent story-appropriate material when they cannot recall what they were told. These authors, as well as Stein and Glenn (1979), report that children are much better able to remember material in canonical order; indeed, Mandler (1979) points out that the younger the child the more dependent he or she is on receiving well-ordered material. Finally, Mandler, Scribner, Cole, and DeForest (1980) obtained identical patterns of recall in children and adults in this country and in Liberia. In the latter case, it did not matter whether the children were schooled or whether the adults were literate.

Smiley and Brown (1979) gave subjects classification materials that could be sorted thematically or taxonomically. Preferences for sorting materials into thematic as opposed to taxonomic groupings showed a curvilinear relationship across age: Preschool children and older adults preferred thematic categories. In follow-up tasks that required subjects to sort another way or showed the experimenter first modeling a taxonomic solution it was established that these were only preferences. Hence, there is evidence that young children's tendencies to produce arrays that tell stories may be due in part to their greater preference for organizations that rely on spatial or temporal relations, rather than to an inability to use organization according to classes.

Wholistic as Opposed to Analytic Responses to Stimuli. There is yet another kind of competing structural tendency that has been suggested as a possible source of interference; this is to respond to stimuli in an integral or wholistic fashion. Smith and Kemler (1978) found that young children do not typically analyze stimuli into the dimensions represented in the stimulus. Thus children compare stimuli on the basis of overall similarity rather than on common values of a specific criteria. This is akin to comparing people not on the basis of hair color but instead on the basis of what they "sort of look like."

If young children are disinclined to analyze stimuli in terms of component dimensions, then it is hardly surprising if they are disinclined to apply a hierarchical classification scheme in a sorting task. To do the latter the child must select criteria that are common to subclasses of objects and that distinguish the subclasses from each other.

I point out that I have characterized the young child as disinclined to analyze stimuli—not as unable to. As Kemler and Smith (1979) point out, it is possible to show that young children can employ a dimensional structure of stimuli but that such access is limited to specific conditions. The notion of access has come to play a central role in current theorizing about the nature of cognitive development. I bring this to your attention here and will return to it.

The Function of Classification Structures

If hierarchical classification structures are inaccessible or likely to lose out to competing structures, why does the young child have them at all? One answer is that these structures facilitate syntax acquisition (Fodor, 1972). Keil (1981) offers another likely answer, at least with regard to the claim that humans are constrained to organize their ontological knowledge in a hierarchical fashion. Children learn words at a phenomenal rate (Carey, 1978), but why this is so has been puzzling. According to Keil, childrens' knowledge of predicates is such that if children hear "the gub is sorry" they can infer that whatever gubs are they move on their own, eat, sleep, and so forth. In short, children can know a lot about what "gub" does and does not mean. Carey's results (Note 3) support this conclusion. She taught preschool children that a given animal (for example, a dog or a human) had a "spleen." Children were then asked whether each of a series of objects such as an aardvark, a fish, a bug, or a mechanical monkey, had one. Whereas children's willingness to grant this organ to other animals depended somewhat upon the similarity of that animal to a dog or human, they never attributed the spleen to inanimate objects.

Access

I draw attention to the fact that the situations in which young children reveal their competencies with hierarchical classification schemes are natural situations in which children go about the normal business of developing language abilities and learning about objects in everyday life. Perhaps we uncover hierarchical classification capacities in these domains because these are the domains within which we were programmed to use these capacities. To explicate, consider Rozin's account of cognitive development.

Rozin (1976) proposed that part of cognitive development involves an increasing ability to access underlying cognitive and perceptual abilities (see Fodor, 1972, 1975, for a similar view). Early and possibly innate abilities are used in only a few or even just one domain. But as development progresses, these abilities are used in more and more settings because of a growing ability to gain access to underlying competencies. Rozin discusses two kinds of access. One is the kind just considered—the ability to employ a given computational system outside of its original evolutionary or ontogenetic domain, independent of whether the routine is used consciously. The other kind of access is the ability to articulate the nature of the principles that underlie behavior. This latter ability is often called metacognition (Flavell & Wellman, 1977; Gleitman, Gleitman, & Shipley, 1972). Pylyshyn (1978) makes a similar distinction between flexible and reflected access. Both are said to result from the development of the access ability.

Situations wherein young children can be shown to use hierarchical classification schemes are predominantly those that do not require the child to access the structure and put it to work in the name of some task demands. It is also noteworthy that situations requiring access, such as list learning or standard classification tasks, are those with which children do poorly. Such observations have led Brown, Bransford, Ferrara, and Campione (1983), Carey (in press), and Mandler (1983) to conclude that part of what develops in the domain of classification skill is due to access—in both of the senses spelled out by Rozin and Pylyshyn. All theorists maintain that conscious access to, or metacognition about, classification structures is a relatively late development (Flavell & Wellman, 1977). Brown and Mandler also focus on the gradual increase in the flexible use of classification. Later in this essay we shall hear more of the idea that with development comes increased ability to access, and so unleash the underlying cognitive and perceptual competencies.

A Return to the Traditional Findings

We researchers have come a long way in our pursuit of an explanation of the nature and development of hierarchical classification structures. We believe that these are available at a very early age and serve to organize acquisition of knowledge about ontological categories and about vocabulary. In pursuit of the answer to why hierarchical structures might not be elicited in traditional classification tasks, we discovered that young children also have available other structures that they use to organize their knowledge. These include collections, scripts, story grammars, and other schemata. We have also uncovered some insights about the nature of what does develop, including the knowledge base, wider access to reasoning principles originally employed only in sharply restricted domains, and metacognition.

Early Number Knowledge

Because number concepts are abstract concepts, they are late to develop—or so reasoned many who wrote about the development of number concepts. But however compelling such reasoning might be, it is surely wrong. It now seems that the ability to count and do simple arithmetic problems may be as natural as the ability to speak a language.

I have already said that preschoolers have a number invariance scheme, by which they correctly classify number-relevant and number-irrelevant transformations. Thus children treat addition and subtraction as operations that alter the value of a set and operations like rearrangement, lengthening, and item substitution, as ones that do not. What I did not say is that they use counting as an algorithm when solving the problems they confront in the magic tasks as well as in other versions of addition and subtraction tasks (Groen & Resnick, 1977; Ginsburg, 1977; Siegler & Robinson, 1982; Starkey & Gelman, 1981).

The conclusion that preschoolers use a counting algorithm to solve addition and subtraction problems may be surprising. You might think that when children count they simply recite the count words from rote memory. But they do not. They have considerable implicit knowledge of the principles that govern counting. Gelman and Gallistel (1978) concluded that preschoolers' understanding of counting is governed by five principles:

1. the one-one principle—every item in a display should be tagged with one and only one unique tag
2. the stable order principle—the tags must be ordered in the same sequence across trials
3. the cardinal principle—the last tag used in a count sequence is the symbol for the number of items in the set
4. the abstraction principle—any kinds of objects can be collected together for purposes of a count
5. the order-irrelevance principle—the objects in a set may be tagged in any sequence as long as the other counting principles are not violated.

Very young children honor these principles in their counting but do not articulate them—that is, they have little or no metacognitive access to them.

Gelman and Meck (1983), while looking for other performances in which children employ these counting principles, reasoned that if preschoolers know the counting principles, they should recognize counting errors. Separate studies tested for their ability to monitor a puppet's application of the one-one, stable-order, and cardinal principles. Error trials in the one-one experiment included the puppet skipping an item. In some trials of the stable-order experiment, the puppet used a list wherein the conventional order of two tags was reversed (e.g., 1, 2, 4, 3, 5, 6). In the cardinal task, in response to the question "How many is that?" the puppet sometimes gave an answer of one greater than the correct number or even some irrelevant property of the last object tagged. Test trials used set sizes ranging from 5 to 20. The larger sets were substantially greater than these young children could count accurately.

The children did very well at declaring trials correct or incorrect in all studies and on all set sizes. For example, in the cardinal task, after the puppet counted and then answered the "how many?" question, children were asked if they wanted to change the puppet's answer whenever they said the puppet was wrong. The 4-year-olds attempted to correct 90% of the puppet's error trials and 93% of these attempts were correct. The 3-year-olds attempted a correction on 70% of the puppet error trials and 94% of these were correct! Thus very young children use the counting principles to judge the counting of others.

I turn now to my claim that the ability to count and do simple arithmetic tasks is universal. First, it appears that most cultures do use a counting procedure. It was once commonplace to assign "primitive" numerical abilities to those from nonliterate cultures (Menninger, 1969). Zaslavsky's (1973) work shows, however, that Africans do count and have done so for centuries. A failure to recognize this was due in part to a failure to realize that one does not have to count with words that are reserved solely for that purpose. Saxe (1979) provides a relevant case in point. He reports that the Papua in New Guinea use the names of their fingers and successive parts of their arms and torso as counting tags. This system is illustrated in Figure 2.

Ginsburg (1981) shows that unschooled children of the Dioula (a West African group) know informal mathematics at a comparable level to that of preschoolers in this country. For example, these un-schooled African children use comparable counting strategies to solve simple arithmetic problems with concrete objects.

Starkey, Spelke, and Gelman (in press) have determined that 6-month-old babies can respond intermodally to numerical information. Infants in their studies were shown slides of two- and three-item displays made up of a heterogeneous collection of common household objects such as a comb, cup, glass, sponge, and so on. On each trial, one slide of each set size was displayed side by side. Between the two slides a loud speaker emitted the sound of two or three drum beats. Incredibly enough, babies had a significant tendency to look to the slide that had the same number of objects as there were drum beats. Prior work by Strauss and Curtis (1981) and by Starkey, Spelke, and Gelman (Note 4) showed that babies abstracted number across heterogeneous visual displays like those used in the intermodal study. It seems that they can also do so across the visual and auditory mode.

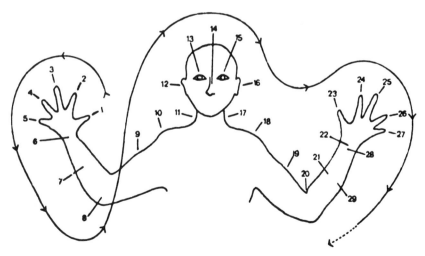

Figure 2. Illustration of the body-part counting sequence used in Papua, New Guinea. Based on a diagram from Saxe (1979). Reprinted by permission.

I confess that I do not have an account of why babies bother to attend to numerical information. Because they do, weight is given to the conclusion that number is a natural domain of cognition.

Development of Counting-Based Knowledge

Narrowing the Gap Between Competence and Performance

When preschool children do the counting themselves, their accuracy falls off rapidly around set size 5. Gelman and Meck's failure to find an effect of set size when children judge the counting of a puppet is the exception to the rule that young children's prowess with numerical tasks is limited to small set sizes (Descouedres, 1947; Gelman & Gallistel, 1978; Schaeffer, Eggelston, & Scott, 1974). Why the difference?

In the error detection tasks children did not have to generate the counting performance, they only had to monitor for conformance to the principles. When counting on their own, children have to keep track of which items have been and have yet to be counted, generate the count list, coordinate the recitation of tags with the pointing to or touching of each item, and remember to repeat the last tag to indicate the cardinal value of the set. Removal of these performance demands had a profound effect, confirming our view that the young child needs to practice counting in order to achieve skill in applying the principles. Like others (e.g., Shiffrin & Dumais, 1981), we are of the view that practice serves to automatize—in this case, the act of counting. The result of practice is that children not only count without error, they count larger set sizes and better remember the goal of determining the last tag. In other words, part of what develops is skill in dealing with the host of performance demands that we all encounter.

The idea that gaps between competence and performance are traceable partly to the lack of automatization of requisite skills figures centrally in several accounts of cognitive development. Case (1974, 1981) and Pascual-Leone (1970) talk of the limits of M-space or working memory and how these limits restrict the number of items in a task or the number of structures a child can work with at once. Shatz (1978) showed that many of the preschoolers' difficulties on communication tasks are due to the performance demands of these tasks. All of these theorists argue that processing space is freed up as a child becomes facile with the responses required. For further discussion of the role of information-processing constraints in cognitive development, see Siegler (1983) and Sternberg and Davidson (in press).

Induction of New Principles

Practice is not the only way one circumvents processing constraints. We also get around memory constraints by imposing organizations on the material we have to remember. If the difficulty of learning to count from 3 to 20 were any predictor of the difficulty of learning to count from 20 to 1,000, it is a safe bet that very few humans would ever learn to count to 1,000. But humans never construct a list of 1,000 number words by brute force. They invariably fasten on a generative scheme involving one or more number generating bases (Zaslavsky, 1973). Such schemes permit the generation of indefinitely long lists of tags by the lawful combination of the relatively few tags in the base set. It is the rare preschooler who has caught on to the base structure and hence acquired the ability to count, in principle, forever. The induction of the generative rules does not usually occur until 5 or 6 years of age (Siegler & Robinson, 1982). Given the ability to count to an indefinite number and the proclivity to do so, the child can go on to induce yet another rule, that the numbers never end (Evans & Gelman, Note 5).

From Implicit to Explicit Knowledge

I have been referring to knowledge of the counting principles as implicit knowledge. I mean to say that the young child's knowledge of counting principles is much like his or her knowledge of language. It will be a long time before the child who says "wented," "goed," "undoed," and so forth can explicate the implicit knowledge of the language that governs the production of such overgeneralization errors. With development, at around 5 to 7 years of age, there will emerge metalinguistic, or explicit knowledge of some rules of the language (Gleitman, Gleitman, & Shipley, 1972). Likewise, there is a trend from implicit to explicit knowledge of the counting principles. The work of Saxe, Sicilian, and Schoenfeld, (Note 6) helps illustrate this point for the stable order principle. They had children watch two puppets count, one using the conventional count list and one using the alphabet. It is not until children are school-aged that they are able to say that an errorless sequence involving the alphabet is better than an error-prone sequence with the count words. Why? To do this children have to explicitly realize that the choice of tags is completely arbitrary. Metacognition about the arbitrariness of symbols is well known to be a late development (e.g., Piaget, 1929; Osherson & Markman, 1974/1975). Not too surprisingly then, success on the Saxe et al. task is late as well.

Conservation Revisited

If the young know so much about numbers, why do they reliably fail the number conservation task? The reasons are many, including the way children interpret the task (Donaldson, 1978; Gelman, 1978). I will focus on but one reason why young children fail.

To successfully perform the number conservation task, the child has to know that whenever the items in one set can be placed in one-to-one correspondence with those in another set, both sets have the same number. This is the set-theoretic definition of numerical equivalence and Piaget assumed that it was the foundation of the child's understanding of number. I have argued that this concept of numerical equivalence requires an explicit understanding of one-to-one correspondence whereas numerical equivalence based on counting does not (Gelman, 1982). With counting a child need not realize that the tags used to count one set can be placed in one-to-one correspondence with those used to count another set. If we assume that the conservation task taps the child's explicit understanding of the role of one-to-one correspondence, then the young child's failure to conserve spontaneously is not in conflict with the conclusion that children know much about numbers. It also suggests that were children's attention focused on the role of counting in establishing the equivalence of the cardinal values in pairs of displays, their implicit knowledge of one-to-one correspondence would become explicit and thus they might conserve. This proved to be the case with 3- and 4-year-old children who, after a brief pretesting experience designed to help them establish this equivalence, were able to conserve and to tell us why they did (Gelman, 1982).

Given these findings, a resolution can be made between the results of recent work on number concepts in young children and Piaget's work on conservation. The initial understanding of number is based on the counting principles and not the logic of classes. Since the principle of one-to-one correspondence is implicit in the counting principles, the latter provide the foundation from which an explicit understanding of the logical principle of one-to-one correspondence can be accessed. (Gelman & Gallistel, 1978; Greeno, Riley, & Gelman, Note 7).

Again, then, we see that the pursuit of what does *not*, as well as what *does*, develop has informed our understanding of cognition and cognitive development. Number seems to be a natural domain of human cognition. The development of number understanding involves (a) closing the competence-performance gap, (b) acquiring new rules and principles, and (c) making explicit what was once implicit.

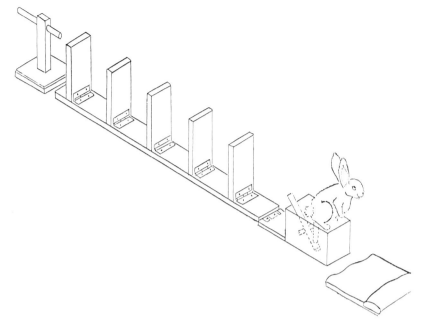

Figure 3. The Fred-the-rabbit apparatus used in the Baillargeon et al. (Note 8) study of causal reasoning in preschoolers.

Causality

In his early studies of the young child's understanding of physical causality, Piaget asked children to explain a variety of natural and mechanical phenomena, for example, the cycle of the moon, floating objects, the movement of clouds, the operation of steam engines and bicycles, and so forth. Analysis of the explanations led Piaget to characterize the young child's thought as fundamentally precausal. Thus he wrote that "immediacy of relations and absence of intermediaries . . . are the two outstanding features of causality around the age of 4–5" (Piaget, 1930, p. 268). The young children in his studies said that the pedals of a bicycle make the wheels turn without being in any way attached to them, that a fire lit alongside an engine makes the wheels of the engine turn—even if it is 2 feet away, and so on.

The idea that an assumption of mechanism is lacking in the preschooler is contradicted by several lines of research. I will share two with you.

Baillargeon, Gelman, and Meck (Note 8) showed 3- and 4-year-old children how a 3-part apparatus worked (illustrated in Figure 3).

The first part was a wooden rod that could be pushed through a hole; the second part was a set of five upright blocks and a lever protruding from a box; and the last part consisted of the lever's box with a toy rabbit (called Fred) sitting on top of the box, which was beside a toy bed. When the rod was pushed through the hole it hit the first block. The first block fell and created a domino effect until the last block fell and depressed the lever. The depression of the lever caused Fred-the-rabbit to fall into his bed. After a working demonstration, the children were asked to predict whether Fred would fall into his bed given variations in different parts of the apparatus. Modifications were of two types: relevant ones, which would disrupt the sequence; and irrelevant ones, which would not. For example, substitution of too short a stick was a relevant change; substitution of a glass tube that could reach the first block was an irrelevant change. Similarly, the removal of one intermediate block was a relevant change; covering an intermediate block with cloth was an irrelevant change. In one experiment, prediction trials were run with a fully visible apparatus. In a second, the intermediate portion of the apparatus was screened.

If young children wrongly believe that the occurrence of the first event in a causal sequence is sufficient to bring about the final event, they should treat all modifications in the apparatus responsible for the first event as potentially disruptive and all modifications of the intermediate part of the apparatus as nondisruptive. On the other hand, if children do understand that the intermediate part of the apparatus and the consequent events effectively connect the first and last events in the sequence, then they should regard only the relevant modifications—whether of the initial or intermediate events—as likely to disrupt the sequence. In the first experiment all children were correct on at least 75% of their 24 predictions. In the second experiment, where the screen blocked the intermediate mechanism, all but one child met the 75% criterion. Differential predictions at this level of accuracy could have occurred only if the children recognized the intermediary events as such.

Shultz (1982) showed that even 2-year-olds assume that a cause produces its effects via a transmission of force, whether directly (as when one ball hits another) or indirectly through an intermediary. In Shultz's experiments children were first shown a cause-effect sequence, for example, the turning on of a blower that extinguished a lighted candle. They were then shown two potential energy sources for the outcome: one white and one green blower, each surrounded on three sides by a plexiglass shield. The critical difference between the two blowers was whether the open side was facing a lighted candle and therefore could blow out the candle. If considerations of mechanism do not influence young children, they should have chosen randomly between the two blowers as cause. They did not. Instead they systematically chose the blower whose opening faced the candle. Similar findings were obtained by transmitting a sound source from a tuning fork and transmitting light from a battery. The consistent result was that children took note of barriers that would stop the transmission of the requisite energy. Of considerable note is that similar results held in Schultz's studies with Mali children in West Africa—whether or not the children were in schooled environments.

My colleagues and I (Bullock, Gelman, & Baillargeon, 1982) have argued that the young child also assumes that causes must precede their effects (the priority principle) and that effects have causes (the principle of weak determinism). To grant these causal principles is not to say that children know that they use them—we doubt that most adults know when they are using these principles. Again, my colleagues and I allow for the implicit use of rules that guide the way the child interacts with his environment without assuming explicit or metacognitive knowledge of these principles.

Again, to say that the young child has some competence is not to say that he or she has a complete, correct understanding of physical causality. As Baillargeon (Note 9) shows, the development of the ability to explain why a prediction is correct evolves very slowly. Even undergraduates at Johns Hopkins University make erroneous assumptions about the way the world works (McCloskey, 1983). Their predictions about how objects will move are more consistent with Aristotle's and the Medievalists' writings on physics than anything Newton ever wrote—never mind Einstein. Wrong theories abound in the history of science, but whatever the theory, assumptions must have been made about priority, mechanism, and determinism or there could hardly be a history of science. Like Carey (in press), we hold that Piaget's experiments on causal reasoning should be viewed as experiments on the acquisition and adaptation of an explanation system, on the concept of explanation, and on the notion of what constitutes an explanation (Bullock et al., 1982). When viewed from this perspective, it is possible to allow that there are qualitatively different theories of physical reality as a function of development or schooling. It is not, however, necessary to deny that the young or uneducated have causal attitudes that are governed by implicit principles of causal reasoning.

There is much more early competence than once assumed. Converging cross-cultural findings point to the fact that there are natural, universal domains of cognition. The whats of development are many, including an expanding knowledge base, an increasing skill at applying existing competencies, an ability to access in some domains and apply them to another, and metacognition. Elsewhere I have argued that these natural competencies guide development within their domain. This brings me to the "how" of cognitive development.

Assimilation and Accommodation

Brown et al. (in press) point out that studies of children's learning during the past decade have emphasized the learner as an active rather than passive recipient of environmental input. Indeed, I should note that the same is true of the study of adult learning and cognition. Theorists like Bransford (1979), Marshall and Morton (1978), and Rumelhart and Ortony (1977) have drawn attention to the need to give the learner schemas that serve as sources for monitoring his or her learning as well as for determining what an individual will perceive. I like to think of these theoretical developments as the developmentalization of learning theory and cognitive psychology. For within the context of developmental theories—particularly Piaget's and Werner's—the learner was always an active, controlling participant in the process of learning (see White, 1970, for a review of genetic theories of learning).

My readers may recall the key concepts in Piagetian theory—assimilation, accommodation, and equilibration. Simply put, assimilation is the incorporation of external stimuli into existing schemes or structures. The environment is structured by, or adjusted to, the individual. In accommodation, the individual's schemes adjust themselves to the demands of the environment. Furthermore, Piaget postulated that every structure tends to "feed" itself, that is, to incorporate into itself external elements that are compatible with its nature. The child's schemes are thus seen as constituting the motivational source, or the "motor" of development. Schemes do not merely constrain the nature and range of exchanges children have with the environment; schemes actively bring about such exchanges in their efforts to "feed" or "actualize" themselves. In Piaget's view then, children's activities are necessary in that they help provide input to children's schemes. In short, assimilation and accommodation are the processes that allow children to self-regulate learning and development. In the next section of this essay I focus on why, despite the vagueness of ideas about self-regulation, they are necessary to an account of how development proceeds.

Gelman and Gallistel (1978) argued that the counting principles constitute a scheme that assimilates and accomodates, guides and motivates development. Consider the case of a 2½-year-old child who said, "2, 6, 10, 16," when engaging in what appeared to be counting. When shown one object and asked how many there were, the child said, "Two." When shown two objects and asked how many there were the child said, "2, 6, 6" (emphasis on the last digit). Finally, when shown three objects and asked to count them the child said, "Ten." This child can be said to have applied all of the how-to-count principles because one unique tag was assigned to each object, the same list was used over trials, and the last tag was repeated in a count to indicate the cardinal number. Obviously the counting principles structured and guided the child's counting performance. The child certainly did not hear anyone count like this.

The children who use nonconventional or idiosyncratic count lists (my favorite is 1, 2, 3, 4, 5, 6, 7, H, I, J) do not do so because they have been taught to use them or have heard them. They must have created these lists using whatever they could find in the environment. In our culture the two obvious candidate lists are the alphabet and the counting numbers. The creation of these nonconventional lists points to the presence of a scheme that requires the count list to have a stable order, but leaves unspecified the nature of the items that constitute the list. What we have then is a principle in search of a list. The principle assimilates items that have a stable order.

Another source of evidence that the counting scheme serves a motivating function is that young children appear to have a compulsion to count, be it cows they pass while in a car, or toys, candies, leaves on a tree, and so on. Because young children are not instructed to practice counting, a theory based on extrinsic motivation would be on shaky grounds. But if we allow that the motivation comes from the structure itself, that is, that the structure prompts the child to assimilate stimuli that are compatible with the structure, then the child's motivation to count can be easily explained.

Children who use an idiosyncratic count list will have to give it up and learn the conventional one, otherwise they will not be understood by others. That is, they must accommodate and adjust their principles to the demands of the environment. I recently came across an example of accommodation in action. A.E., a 24-month-old precocious counter, had been in the habit of practicing her count list: "1, 2, 3, 4, 5, 6, 8, 9, 10." For some time, and to no avail, her mother had been pointing out that she left out the 7. But later the child was overheard to say "1, 2, 3, 4, 5, 6, 8, 9, 10—where's the 7?" For a week thereafter, A.E. counted only up to 6, as if to indicate that she knew she had to make a change. Finally, A.E. resumed counting past 6, with 7 in the list.

Saxe (1982) has documented another example of the accommodation and development of a count list. Earlier I referred to the body-part list used by the Papua in New Guinea. Until recently the list had 53 entries with no base rules. But after coming into contact with Australian currency, the Papua started to use a base-20. The source of the base accommodation was probably the currency; the motivation was probably the necessity for the Papua to find a way to deal with the large numbers involved in cash transactions.

There is much work to do in filling in the account of how the counting principles constrain and guide the acquisition of their development. I am concerned that we researchers cannot do the job without notions like self-regulation. Indeed, I believe this is true for many developmental phenomena.

The literature on language acquisition is full of examples of young children monitoring their utterances and correcting some of their errors (Clark & Clark, 1977). Weir (1962) documented the strong tendency of beginning language learners to lay awake at night and practice the sentences and words they learned during the day. Students of motor development have also drawn attention to the effort the young put into practicing and rehearsing their new-found skills without any external feedback (Bruner, 1973). The work of Deloache and Brown (cited in Brown et al., 1983) makes it clear that the same is true when toddlers have to remember where they have left something.

Deloache and Brown devised a version of hide-and-seek in which children aged 18 to 23 months were required to find a toy hidden in a room—behind a chair, under a pillow, inside a closet, and so on. However, they had to wait for some time after the experimenter baited the hidden site. They actively worked at remembering where the attractive toy was; they tended to verbalize about the toy or its hiding place, to look toward the hiding place, to point to the hiding place, to peek, and so on.

To say that there is a ubiquitous tendency for young learners to self-regulate only begins to account for development. For one thing, there are developments within the domain of self-regulation. For another thing, assimilation and accommodation (and related processes) are not the only developmental processes at work; at least two other powerful processes are differentiation and integration. To do justice to these topics, I would need to write yet another essay. Hence, I refer you to the work of Eleanor Gibson (1967) and Keil (1981) on differentiation, and to others like Fischer (1980), Siegler and Klahr (1982), and Rumelhart and Norman (1978) for ideas about integration. For now, I simply acknowledge that there are developments in the domain of self-regulation, which might seem to raise a contradiction between two conclusions I have reached. These are that even very young children regulate their learning yet lack metacognitions (see also Flavell & Wellman, 1977).

In Piaget's letter writings on assimilation, accommodation, and equilibration, he distinguished between autonomous, active, and conscious regulation. The examples about counting and language use illustrate autonomous regulation. Active regulation is said to occur when the learner constructs and tests theories as she or he tries to make sense of the world. Finally, conscious regulation is just that— the explicit invention, modification, and testing of theories about the world of objects and about the mind. For Piaget, each level of regulation emerged out of the former and hence represented progress in the development of the self-regulation function.

Karmiloff-Smith and Inhelder (1974/75) demonstrate the difference between autonomous and active regulation. They studied the way in which children figured out how to balance varieties of blocks: standard blocks, blocks glued on top of each other, blocks with hidden weights, and blocks that were hollow. With their application of brute force and the resulting proprioceptive feedback, preschoolers balanced blocks rather well. Their persistence and their use of trial and error reflects autonomous regulation. Somewhat older children developed a theory that the blocks balanced at their geometric center. This was true only for the nontrick blocks; applied to the trick blocks the theory would fail. The older children did fail where the young did not, by insisting on following their new-found theory. Hence their conclusion that it was impossible to balance certain blocks. These impossible blocks were set aside as exceptions to the rule—even when, with their eyes closed, they succeeded in balancing them (because they relied on proprioceptive feedback). Armed with this theory, the children continued to try balancing blocks. Eventually, they began to worry about the growing number of exceptions to their theory. They then invented a local exception rule. But eventually the exception rule, too, began to trouble them and so they began to search for a reconciliation of their theories, thus giving evidence of conscious regulation.

The Piagetian work on levels of self-regulation makes clear that there is no contradiction between the conclusions that metacognition is late to develop and that self-monitoring is a ubiquitous feature of very early learning. Piaget's work also underscores Brown et al.'s (in press) conclusion that there is a real need for those who study learning and development to make a conceptual distinction between self-monitoring and metacognition. Not only is one earlier to develop than the other, but these are different activities. Monitoring is an on-line, ever-present, and integral part of intellectual functioning. Metacognition involves having explicit knowledge both of this functioning and of the nature and content of knowledge.

The work by Karmiloff-Smith and Inhelder adds weight to the conclusion that much of cognitive development is self-motivated. In their experiments, no one ever told the child that he or she had an inadequate theory, or indeed that organization was needed to balance the blocks. To Karmiloff-Smith (1979) the child's independent actions reflect a motive to systematize and come to know the very structure that guides the regulation in the first place. Bowerman's (1982) work on semantic development and Newport's (1980) work on the acquisition of sign buttress this conclusion.

Newport found that deaf children of first generation signers acquire a more richly structured language than do their parents. There must be an internally driven motivation to come to know and systematize the structure. How else can the fact that the children take their parents' input and rework it in the absence of any models be explained? Bowerman found that during the initial period of sentence production young children use the transitive causal verbs of bring and drop correctly. Then toward the end of their second birthday they switch to saying things like "I come it closer so it won't fall." They also say things like "untie it off," and "are you gonna nice yourself?" (meaning to make pretty with makeup). Bowerman argues that children go from using a local rule to a more general one—in this case about the semantics of causatives. The important fact here is that the local rule allows children to communicate adequately. Hence, their changing to other devices is most readily accounted for by postulating the children's need to master structure.

I draw your attention to a feature that is common to both the Bowerman and Karmiloff-Smith work. Initially a child will do something right; then without any apparent reason, will start to do it wrong. Development is not just a matter of practicing at doing better what is already done right; there is also a tendency to master the system, even if it means living with doing it wrong (cf. Strauss, 1982).

In summation, a major feature of recent theorizing about the how of cognitive development is the granting of an active role to the learner. No one has concluded that all learning and development comes from within, just that a reasonable amount does.

Reference Notes

1. Baillargeon, R. *Object permanence in the five-month-old infant.* Paper presented at the International Conference on Infant Studies, Austin, March 1982.

2. Mandler, J. M. *Representation and retrieval in infancy.* Paper delivered at Conference on Infant Memory, Mississauga, Canada, May 1982.

3. Carey, S. *The child's concept of animal.* Paper presented at Psychonomic Society, San Antonio, TX, 1978.

4. Starkey, P., Spelke, E., & Gelman, R. *Number competences in infants: Sensitivity to numeric invariance and numeric change.* Paper presented at the International Conference on Infant Studies, New Haven, CT, 1980.

5. Evans, D., & Gelman, R. *Understanding infinity: A beginning inquiry.* Unpublished manuscript, University of Pennsylvania, 1982.

6. Saxe, G. B., Sicilian, S., & Schonfield, I. *Developmental differences in children's understanding of conventional properties of counting.* Unpublished manuscript, The Graduate Center of the City University of New York, 1981.

7. Greeno, J. G., Riley, M. S., & Gelman, R. *Young children's counting and understanding of principles.* Unpublished manuscript, University of Pittsburgh and University of Pennsylvania, 1983.

8. Baillargeon, R., Gelman, R., & Meck, E. *Are preschoolers truly indifferent to causal mechanism?* Paper presented at the bi-annual meeting of The Society for Research in Child Development, Boston, April 1981.

9. Baillargeon, R. *Young children's understanding of causal mechanism.* Unpublished dissertation, University of Pennsylvania, 1981.

References

Bartlett, F. C. *Thinking: An experimental and social study.* New York: Basic Books, 1932.

Biederman, I. On the semantics of a glance at a scene. In M. Kubovy & J. R. Pomerantz (Eds.), *Perceptual organization.* Hillsdale, NJ: Erlbaum, 1982.

Bower, G. H., Black, J. B., & Turnure, T. J. Scripts in memory for test. *Cognitive Psychology,* 1979, *11,* 177–220.

Bowerman, M. Starting to talk worse: Clues to language acquisition from children's late speech errors. In S. Strauss (Ed.), *U-shaped behavioral growth.* New York: Academic Press, 1982.

Bransford, J. D. *Human cognition: Learning, understanding, and remembering.* Belmont, CA: Wadsworth, 1979.

Brown, A. L., Bransford, J. D., Ferrara, R. A., & Campione, J. C. Learning, remembering, and understanding. In J. H. Flavell & E. M. Markman (Eds.), *Handbook of child psychology: Vol. 3. Cognitive development* (4th ed.). New York: Wiley, 1983.

Bruner, J. S. Organization of early skilled action. *Child Development,* 1973, *44,* 1–11.

Bruner, J. S., & Olver, R. R. Development of equivalence transformations in children. In J. C. Wright & J. Kagan (Eds.), Basic cognitive processes in children. *Monographs of the Society for Research in Child Development,* 1963, *28* (2, Serial No. 86).

Bullock, M., Gelman, R., & Baillargeon, R. The development of causal reasoning. In J. Friedman (Ed.), *The developmental psychology of time.* New York: Academic Press, 1982.

Carey, S. The child as word learner. In M. Halle, J. Brennan, & G. A. Miller (Eds.), *Linguistic theory and psychological reality.* Cambridge: Massachusetts Institute of Technology Press, 1978.

Carey, S. Are children fundamentally different kinds of thinkers and learners than adults? In S. Chipman, J. Segal, & R. Glaser, (Eds.), *Thinking and learning skills* (Vol. 2). Hillsdale, NJ: Erlbaum, in press.

Case, R. Structures and strictures: Some functional limitations on the course of cognitive growth. *Cognitive Psychology,* 1974, *6,* 544–573.

Case, R. General developmental influences on the acquisition of elementary concepts and algorithms in arithmetic. In T. P. Carpenter, J. M. Moser, & T. A. Romberg, (Eds.), *Addition and subtraction: A cognitive perspective.* Hillsdale, NJ: Erlbaum, 1981.

Chi, M. T. H., & Koeske, R. D. Network representation of a child's dinosaur knowledge. *Developmental Psychology,* 1983, *19,* 29–39.

Clark, E. J. Meanings and concepts. In J. H. Flavell & E. M. Markman, (Eds.), *Handbook of child psychology: Vol. 3. Cognitive development* (4th ed.). New York: Wiley, 1983.

Clark, H. H., & Clark, E. V. *Psychology and language: An introduction to psycholinguistics.* New York: Harcourt Brace Jovanovich, 1977.

Descouedres, A. *Le Développement de l'enfant de deux à septs ans.* Neuchâtel, Delachaux et Niestlè, 1947.

Donaldson, M. *Children's minds.* New York: Norton, 1978.

Fischer, K. W. A theory of cognitive development. *Psychological Review,* 1980, *87,* 477–525.

Flavell, J. H. *The developmental psychology of Jean Piaget.* Princeton, NJ: Van Nostrand, 1963.

Flavell, J. H., & Wellman, H. M. Metamemory. In R. V. Kail, Jr. & J. W. Hagen (Eds.), *Perspectives on the development of memory and cognition.* Hillsdale, NJ: Erlbaum, 1977.

Fodor, J. A. Some reflections on L. S. Vygotsky's thought and language. *Cognition,* 1972, *1,* 83–95.

Fodor, J. A. *The language of thought.* New York: Thomas Y. Crowell, 1975.

Gelman, R. Logical capacity of very young children. *Child Development*, 1972, *43*, 371–383.

Gelman, R. Cognitive development. In M. R. Rosenzweig & L. W. Porter (Eds.), *Annual review of psychology* (Vol. 29). Palo Alto, CA: Annual Reviews, 1978.

Gelman, R. Accessing one-to-one correspondence: Still another paper about conservation. *British Journal of Psychology*, 1982, *73*, 209–220.

Gelman, R., & Baillargeon, R. A review of some Piagetian concepts. In J. H. Flavell & E. M. Markman (Eds.), *Handbook of Child Psychology: Vol. 3. Cognitive development* (4th ed.). New York: Wiley, 1983.

Gelman, R., & Gallistel, C. R. *The child's understanding of number.* Cambridge, MA: Harvard University Press, 1978.

Gelman, R., & Meck, E. Preschooler's counting: Principles before skill? *Cognition*, 1983, *13*, 343–359.

Gelman, R., & Spelke, E. The development of thoughts about animate and inanimate objects: Implications for research on social cognition. In J. H. Flavell & L. Ross (Eds.), *Social cognitive development: Frontiers and possible futures.* Cambridge, England: Cambridge University Press, 1981.

Gibson, E. J. *Principles of perceptual learning and development.* New York: Appleton-Century-Crofts, 1967.

Gibson, E. J. The concept of affordances in development: The renascence of functionalism. In W. A. Collins (Ed.), *Minnesota Symposium on Child Psychology* (Vol. 15). Hillsdale, NJ: Erlbaum, 1982.

Ginsburg, H. P. *Children's arithmetic.* New York: Van Nostrand Reinhold, 1977.

Ginsburg, H. P. The development of addition in the contexts of culture, social class and race. In T. P. Carpenter, J. M. Moser, & T. A. Romberg (Eds.), *Addition and subtraction: A developmental perspective.* Hillsdale, NJ: Erlbaum, 1981.

Ginsburg, H. P. & Opper, S. *Piaget's theory of intellectual development* (2nd ed.). Englewood Cliffs, NJ: Prentice-Hall, 1979.

Gleitman, L. R., Gleitman, H., & Shipley, E. F. The emergence of the child as grammarian. *Cognition*, 1972, *1*, 137–164.

Groen, G., & Resnick, L. B. Can preschool children invent addition algorithms? *Journal of Educational Psychology*, 1977, *69*, 645–52.

Gruber, H. E., & Vonèche, J. J. *The essential Piaget: An interpretative reference and guide.* London: Routledge & Kegan Paul, 1977.

Inhelder, B., & Piaget, J. *The early growth of logic in the child.* New York: Harper & Row, 1964.

Karmiloff-Smith, A. Micro- and macro-developmental changes in language acquisition and other representational systems. *Cognitive Science*, 1979, *3*, 91–118.

Karmiloff-Smith, A., & Inhelder, B. If you want to get ahead, get a theory. *Cognition*, 1974/75, *3*, 195–212.

Keil, F. C. *Semantic and conceptual development.* Cambridge, MA: Harvard University Press, 1979.

Keil, F. C. Constraints on knowledge and cognitive development. *Psychological Review*, 1981, *88*, 197–227.

Kemler, D. G., & Smith, L. B. Accessing similarity and dimensional relations: The effects of integrality and separability on the discovery of relational concepts. *Journal of Experimental Psychology: General*, 1979, *108*, 133–150.

Mandler, J. M. Categorical and schematic organization in memory. In C. R. Puff (Ed.), *Memory organization and structure.* New York: Academic Press, 1979.

Mandler, J. M. Structural invariants in development. In L. S. Liben (Ed.), *Piaget and the foundations of knowledge.* Hillsdale, NJ: Erlbaum, 1981.

Mandler, J. M. Representation. In J. H. Flavell & E. M. Markman (Eds.), *Handbook of child psychology: Vol. 3. Cognitive development* (4th ed.). New York: Wiley, 1983.

Mandler, J. M., & Johnson, N. S. Remembrance of things parsed: Story structure and recall. *Cognitive Psychology,* 1977, *9,* 111–151.

Mandler, J. M., & Parker, R. E. Memory for descriptive and spatial information in complex pictures. *Journal of Experimental Psychology: Human Learning and Memory,* 1976, *2,* 38–48.

Mandler, J. M. Scribner, S., Cole, M., & DeForest, M. Cross-cultural invariance in story recall. *Child Development,* 1980, *51,* 19–26.

Markman, E. M. Two different principles of conceptual organization. In M. E. Lamb & A. L. Brown (Eds.), *Advances in developmental psychology* (Vol. 1). Hillsdale, NJ: Erlbaum, 1981.

Markman, E. M., & Callahan, M. A. An analysis of hierarchical classification. In R. Sternberg (Ed.), *Advances in the psychology of human intelligence* (Vol. 2). Hillsdale, NJ: Erlbaum, in press.

Markman, E. M., Horton, M. S., & McLanahan, A. G. Classes and collections: Principles of organization in the learning of hierarchical relations. *Cognition,* 1980, *8,* 227–241.

Markman, E. M., & Siebert, J. Classes and collections: Internal organization and resulting holistic properties. *Cognitive Psychology,* 1976, *8,* 561–577.

Marshall, J. C., & Morton, J. On the mechanics of Emma. In A. Sinclair, R. J. Jarvella, & W. J. M. Levelt (Eds.), *The child's conception of language.* New York: Springer-Verlag, 1978.

McCloskey, M. Naive theories of motion. In D. Gentner & A. L. Stevens (Eds.), *Mental models.* Hillsdale, NJ: Erlbaum, in press.

Menninger, K. *Number words and number symbols.* Cambridge: Massachusetts Institute of Technology Press, 1969.

Nelson, K. & Gruendel, J. Generalized event representations: Basic building blocks of cognitive development. In A. L. Brown & M. E. Lamb (Eds.), *Advances in developmental psychology.* Hillsdale, NJ: Erlbaum, 1981.

Newport, E. L. Constraints on structure: Evidence from American sign language and language learning. In W. A. Collins (Ed.), *Minnesota Symposium on Child Psychology* (Vol. 14). Hillsdale, NJ: Erlbaum, 1980.

Osherson, D. N., & Markman, E. M. Language and the ability to evaluate contradictions and tautologies. *Cognition,* 1974/75, *3,* 213–226.

Pascual-Leone, J. A mathematical model for the transition rule in Piaget's development stages. *Acta Psychologica,* 1970, *63,* 301–345.

Piaget, J. *The child's conception of the world.* London: Routledge and Kegan Paul, 1929.

Piaget, J. *The child's conception of physical causality.* London: Routledge & Kegal Paul, 1930.

Piaget, J. *The construction of reality.* New York: Basic Books, 1954.

Poulsen, D., Kintsch, E., Kintsch, W., & Premack, D. Children's comprehension and memory for stories. *Journal of Experimental Child Psychology,* 1979, *28,* 379–403.

Pylyshyn, Z. W. When is attribution of beliefs justified? *Behavioral and Brain Sciences,* 1978, *1,* 592–593.

Rozin, P. The evolution of intelligence and access to the cognitive unconscious. In J. M. Sprague & A. D. Epstein (Eds.), *Progress in psychobiology and physiological psychology* (Vol. 6). New York: Academic Press, 1976.

Rumelhart, D. E., & Norman, D. A. Accretion, tuning and restructuring: Three modes of learning. In J. W. Cotton & R. Klatzky (Eds.), *Semantic factors in cognition.* Hillsdale, NJ: Erlbaum, 1978.

Rumelhart, D. E., & Norman, D. A. Analogical processes in learning. In J. R. Anderson (Ed.), *Cognitive skills and their acquisition*. Hillsdale, NJ: Erlbaum, 1981.

Rumelhart, D. E., & Ortony, A. The representation of knowledge in memory. In R. C. Anderson, R. J. Spiro, & W. E. Montague (Eds.), *Schooling and the acquisition of knowledge*. Hillsdale, NJ: Erlbaum, 1977.

Saxe, G. B. Children's counting: The early formation of numerical symbols. In D. Wolfe (Ed.), *New directions for child development: Vol. 3. Early symbolization*. San Francisco: Jossey-Bass, 1979.

Saxe, G. B. The changing form of numerical thought as a function of contact with currency among the Oksapmin of Papua New Guinea. *Developmental Psychology*, 1982, *18*, 583–594.

Schaeffer, B., Eggleston, V. H., & Scott, J. L. Number development in young children. *Cognitive Psychology*, 1974, *6*, 357–79.

Schank, R. A., & Abelson, B. *Scripts, plans, goals and understanding*. Hillsdale, NJ: Erlbaum, 1977.

Shatz, M. The relationship between cognitive processes and the development of communication skills. In C. B. Keasey (Ed.), *Nebraska Symposium on Motivation* (Vol. 25). Lincoln: University of Nebraska Press, 1978.

Shiffrin, R. M., & Dumais, S. T. The development of automism. In J. R. Anderson (Ed.). *Cognitive skills and their acquisition*. Hillsdale, NJ: Erlbaum, 1981.

Shultz, T. R. Rules of causal attribution. *Monographs of the Society for Research in Child Development*, 1982, 47(1, Serial No. 194).

Siegler, R. S. Information processing approaches to development. In W. Kessen (Ed.), *Handbook of child psychology: Vol. 11. History, theories and methods* (4th ed.). New York: Wiley, 1983.

Siegler, R. S., & Klahr, D. When do children learn: The relationship between existing knowledge and the ability to acquire new knowledge. In R. Glaser (Ed.), *Advances in instructional psychology*. Hillsdale, NJ: Erlbaum, 1982.

Siegler, R. S., & Robinson, M. The development of numerical understandings. In H. W. Reese & L. P. Lipsitt (Eds.), *Advance in Child Development and Behavior* (Vol. 16). New York: Academic Press, 1982.

Smiley, S. S., & Brown, A. L. Conceptual preference for thematic or taxonomic relations: A nonmonotonic trend for preschool to old age. *Journal of Experimental Child Psychology*, 1979, *28*, 249–257.

Smith, L. B., & Kemler, D. G. Levels of experienced dimensionality in children and adults. *Cognitive Psychology*, 1978, *10*, 502–532.

Sommers, F. Predictability. In M. Black (Ed.), *Philosophy in America*. Ithaca, NY: Cornell University Press, 1965.

Starkey, P., & Gelman, R. The development of addition and subtraction abilities prior to formal schooling. In T. P. Carpenter, J. M. Moser, & T. A. Romberg (Eds.), *Addition and subtraction: A developmental perspective*. Hillsdale, NJ: Erlbaum, 1981.

Starkey, P. D., Spelke, E. S., & Gelman, R. Detection of intermodal numerical correspondences by human infants. *Science*, in press.

Stein, N. L., & Glenn, C. G. An analysis of story comprehension in elementary school children. In R. Freedle (Ed.), *New directions in discourse processing* (Vol. 2). Norwood, NJ: Ablex, 1979.

Stein, N. L., & Trabasso, T. What's in a story: An approach to comprehension and instruction. In R. Glaser (Ed.), *Advances in the psychology of instruction* (Vol. 2). Hillsdale, NJ: Erlbaum, 1982.

Sternberg, R. J., & Davidson, J. E. Competence and performance in intellectual development. In E. Neimark (Ed.), *Modulators of competence*. Hillsdale, NJ: Erlbaum, in press.

Strauss, M. S., & Curtis, L. E. Infant perception of numerosity. *Child Development*, 1981, *52*, 1146–1152.

Strauss, S. (Ed.), *U-shaped behavioral growth*. New York: Academic Press, 1982.

Vygotsky, L. S. *Thought and language*. Cambridge: Massachusetts Institute of Technology Press, 1962.

Weir, R. *Language in the crib*. The Hague: Mouton, 1962.

Werner, H., *Comparative psychology of mental development*. New York: Harper, 1940.

White, S. H. The learning theory tradition for child psychology. In P. H. Mussen (Ed.), *Carmichael's manual of child psychology* (Vol. 1). New York: Wiley, 1970.

Zaslavsky, C. *Africa counts*. Boston: Prindle, Weber & Schmidt, 1973.

COMMENTS

An examination of cognitive development in children necessarily focuses on the development of mental structures, the processes by which this development occurs, and the age-related changes that accompany the child's growing capacity to perform mental operations. Gelman's essay traces the current understanding of how the intellect organizes its structure, and how the child's mental system results from his or her interaction with the environment. Gelman very systematically develops a view of the developmental process based on a detailed presentation of experiments and the conclusions or hypotheses these generate. These conclusions are firmly propelling this branch of psychology toward an increasingly comprehensive view of the maturational changes that influence intellectual growth.

The reader is offered an unusually lucid picture of how one thinker/experimenter's analysis proceeds, which is a corollary to the way this field of psychology proceeds. Thus, the reader is exposed to an explicit model of the kind of thinking, theory-generation, and knowledge-building in which experimental-developmental psychologists engage. The content and the methodology of cognitive development are presented together, an important achievement from a teaching perspective.

Descriptions of experimental inquiries with children invite the instructor to repeat experiments and to think through the types of conclusions that can be reached in several dimensions—from the recapitulations of stage-phenomena to the utilization of hierarchial classification schemes by children. Equally intriguing may be the various experimental methods used to clarify the meaning of previous experimental findings that are contradictory, difficult to interpret, or inadequate.

This material is presented so that the reader learns about the child's mind by learning about the earnest attempts to create experiments that resemble the mental operations under study. This approach offers a window to learning based upon experimental methods rather than the dry presentation of facts derived from studies.

This approach also considers questions about the interrelationship of dimensions such as the role of knowledge and perceptual capacities among children at different ages. An experimental approach that generates questions as well as answers demonstrates a learning-set that may be acquired by the serious student of psychology.

More specifically the Gelman approach attempts to explain several current concepts of cognitive growth, particularly the development of hierarchial classification structures. The reader is challenged